Praise for *Sit Down to Rise Up* and Shelly Tygielski

"[Shelly Tygielski] is saving people's lives ... and giving them hope."
— **President Joe Biden**

"[Shelly Tygielski] is like a superhero whose special superpower is her heart."
— **Arianna Huffington**, bestselling author of *Thrive*

"Shelly Tygielski is the real deal, a force of nature."
— **Dr. Jon Kabat-Zinn**, bestselling author of *Wherever You Go, There You Are*

"The writing is friendly and warm, brimming with energy, imagery, and positivity — and there's nothing fluffy about it. Indeed, this advice stands to be life-changing."
— *Foreword* (starred review)

"Shelly is one of the great mindfulness teachers of our time, a captivating storyteller, and the epitome of what it means to authentically live a heart-based life."
— **davidji**, bestselling author of *Sacred Powers*

"Shelly has proved that one person can bring awe into the life of another, that we can all make a difference, and that asking for help is incredibly brave."
— **Maria Shriver**, award-winning journalist and bestselling author

"This work of heart will change your life as it provides us all with a practical guide to transforming our selves from the inside out to create more collaboration and well-being in our shared world."
— **Daniel J. Siegel, MD**, *New York Times* bestselling author of *Mind*, *Aware*, and *IntraConnected*

"Through Shelly, we're reminded that our weary hearts are more than strong enough to love the world as we love ourselves."
— **Susanna Schrobsdorff**, former *TIME* editor at large

"This is a do-not-miss book for anyone skeptical of the idea of self-care. It will inspire you to show up in ways big and small."
— **Busy Philipps**, award-winning actress and bestselling author

"Shelly's story and her ability to take action will show people how much power they really have. *Sit Down to Rise Up* is for anyone who is ready to heal themselves and help heal the world."
— **Yung Pueblo** (Diego Perez), *New York Times* bestselling author, activist, and influencer

"Shelly is making mindfulness and self-care more accessible to everyone but specifically for individuals who have experienced trauma. In *Sit Down to Rise Up*, she makes the important argument that the inner journey for each person *must* be connected to our actions and words in the outer world for true well-being to emerge."
— **David Simas**, former CEO of the Obama Foundation

"Kindness can be contagious and [Shelly] proved that."
— **Kelly Clarkson**, Grammy Award–winning singer, songwriter, and television host of *The Kelly Clarkson Show*

"In this remarkable new book, Shelly illuminates the ways in which love has become her primary motivation, her guiding principle, and a unifying theme for her revolutionary work as a teacher, writer, and activist....Her book is a gift to its readers and to those they will touch."
— **Bryan Welch**, former CEO of Mindful Communications and *Mindful Magazine*

"From the very first page, Shelly's stories blow you away....If the entire world read this book, we would solve all of our problems, fast. Of all the many mindful voices in the world, Shelly's is one we should be listening to."
— **Justin Michael Williams**, author of *Stay Woke: A Meditation Guide for the Rest of Us*

"A must-read for anyone interested in living a life of meaning, purpose, and service."
— **Rich Fernandez, PhD**, CEO of Search Inside Yourself Leadership Institute

"Shelly has the extraordinary ability to turn confusing, frustrating, even demoralizing moments into opportunities for connection and love. Here she teaches us how to do the same. This book draws on her rare combination of wisdom, warmth, and an extraordinarily practical mind."
— **Jessica Yellin**, award-winning journalist, bestselling author, and founder of News Not Noise

"This book, and Shelly's story, deeply inspired me in the way few self-help books do. Yes, self-care is at its heart, but *Sit Down to Rise Up* transcends our culture's common focus on individual wellness, demonstrating the greater power and purpose in applying these principles to communal care. In doing so, it helps to answer life's central question of 'what are we here for, anyway?'"
— **Emily McDowell**, writer, illustrator, and founder of Em & Friends

"[This] book is all about how to respond to stress in a way that stimulates growth."
— **Next Big Idea Club** (where *Sit Down to Rise Up* was a Fall 2021 Finalist)

"[Shelly] shares what she learned with others so that we can unpack the deep spaces and places in our own minds."
— **Tamron Hall**, *The Tamron Hall Show*

"Shelly Tygielski writes her first book...for all Americans to understand why self-care isn't self-centered, but truly a selfless act."
— *Yoga Magazine*

"Although it would be difficult for most people to recall a year more harrowing and fraught with uncertainty than 2020, there were still some bright spots, thanks to women who decided to press ahead and bring light and hope to their communities. Meet [Shelly] — who went above and beyond the call this year to inspire...and comfort people in need."
— *The Washington Post*

"[Shelly is] a rare example of how embracing fear and using your platform can lead to big-scale, meaningful change."
— *Forbes*

"After the Parkland shooting, Shelly Tygielski was there for my family and our community to offer support, love, and healing. Her embrace of my family and our community continues to this day. This is how she lives her life."

— **Fred Guttenberg**, activist and author of *Find the Helpers*

"*Sit Down to Rise Up* helps us rediscover what we already know to be true: that long-lasting fulfillment in life is inextricably tied to community and purpose. In this book, Shelly Tygielski provides us with the grounding and agency to bring our best selves forward into a world that needs us."

— **Jeff Krasno**, founder of Commune and Wanderlust

"Shelly Tygielski's writing synthesizes deep wisdom, practical science, and direct experience. She clearly illuminates the power of caring for ourselves. The radical self-care she invites us to engage in goes beyond self-centered wellness. It is anchored in a resolve to contribute to our collective well-being."

— **Dr. Angel Acosta**, director of fellowship at the Garrison Institute

"I love this woman! She's transformed my life in so many ways, and once you read this book, she will transform yours, too."

— **Jhoni Marchinko**, Emmy Award–winning screenwriter on *Will & Grace*, *2 Broke Girls*, and *Murphy Brown*

SIT
DOWN
TO
RISE UP

How Radical Self-Care Can
Change the World

SIT
DOWN
TO
RISE UP

Shelly Tygielski

FOREWORD BY **CHELSEA HANDLER**
AFTERWORD BY **SHARON SALZBERG**

New World Library
Novato, California

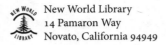 New World Library
14 Pamaron Way
Novato, California 94949

The material in this book is intended for education. It is not meant to take the place of diagnosis and treatment by a qualified medical practitioner or therapist. No expressed or implied guarantee of the effects of the use of the recommendations can be given or liability taken.

Text design by Tona Pearce Myers

Library of Congress Cataloging-in-Publication Data

Names: Tygielski, Shelly, author. | Handler, Chelsea, writer of foreword. | Salzberg, Sharon, writer of afterword.
Title: Sit down to rise up : how radical self-care can change the world / Shelly Tygielski ; foreword by Chelsea Handler ; afterword by Sharon Salzberg.
Description: Novato, California : New World Library, [2021] | Includes bibliographical references. | Summary: "A combination of memoir, manifesto, and how-to guide that shows how mindfulness can be a powerful tool for spurring collective action" -- Provided by publisher.
Identifiers: LCCN 2021031347 (print) | LCCN 2021031348 (ebook) | ISBN 9781608687442 (paperback) | ISBN 9781608687459 (epub)
Subjects: LCSH: Tygielski, Shelly. | Self-actualization (Psychology) | Self-realization. | Mindfulness (Psychology)
Classification: LCC BF637.S4 T94 2021 (print) | LCC BF637.S4 (ebook) | DDC 155.2--dc23
LC record available at https://lccn.loc.gov/2021031347
LC ebook record available at https://lccn.loc.gov/2021031348

Originally published in hardcover by New World Library in 2021
First paperback printing, September 2024
ISBN 978-1-60868-951-4
Ebook ISBN 978-1-60868-952-1
Printed in Canada

New World Library is committed to protecting our natural environment. This book is made of material from well-managed FSC®-certified forests and other controlled sources.

10   9   8   7   6   5   4   3   2   1

MIX
Paper | Supporting
responsible forestry
FSC® C103567
www.fsc.org

For the women who came before me,
who sacrificed, toiled, and made themselves small,
so that I could one day have a voice.

And especially for you, Mom.
I love you.

SCREAM
So that one day
One hundred years from now
Another sister will not have to
Dry her tears wondering
Where in history
She lost her voice.

— JASMINE KAUR

Contents

Part One: SIT DOWN
[The Inner Journey to Me]

Part Two: SHOW UP
[The Outer Journey to We]

Part Three: **RISE UP**
[The Movement to Us]

Preface to the Paperback Edition

In early 2020, I sat down to write a draft of *Sit Down to Rise Up*. Had I finished it prior to March of that year, this book would have looked different. As I was putting pen to paper and spring turned into summer, the world was reeling from the profound impacts of the Covid-19 pandemic. Lockdowns, social distancing, and the pervasive fear of illness and loss had fundamentally altered our daily lives and our perceptions of normalcy. During this time of unprecedented disruption, I sought to explore the concepts of radical self-care, mutual aid, and community resilience as pathways to healing and transformation. Let's just say the principles I outline and (try to) live by were put to the test!

Now, as we prepare this new edition for release, I find myself reflecting on the tumultuous journey humanity has undertaken since I first began writing. The years following 2020 have been marked by a complex tapestry of hope and hopelessness, polarization and unification, triumphs and disappointments. In some way, four years doesn't seem like a long enough period to warrant reflection, and yet, in many ways it seems as if lifetimes have gone by because of all that we have endured. Reading your own work back to yourself (or worse, having someone else quote something you don't even remember writing!) is a strange experience years later. I always worried that my words would not feel relevant beyond the moment that I wrote them. How would the tenets of *Sit Down to Rise Up* hold up four years later … a decade later … fifty years from now?

I finished rereading my book right before sitting to write this preface, and I realized that the themes I chose to explore speak to the inherent trials of being human. They were relevant a hundred years ago and will be relevant still one hundred years from now. We need each other in order to survive. We need each other in order to thrive.

In the wake of the pandemic, amid contentious elections globally, enduring natural disasters, and wars still being waged, I remind myself and you, the reader, that we have witnessed extraordinary acts of kindness and solidarity. Communities have come together in remarkable ways, demonstrating that self-care and mutual aid are not just concepts but a shared reality. We have seen strangers supporting one another, grassroots organizations stepping in where traditional systems have faltered, and individuals taking bold actions to care for their communities and themselves. This period has underscored the immense power of collective action and the deep reservoirs of compassion that exist within us.

Yet, alongside these heartening examples, we have also faced significant challenges. These past four years have exposed and exacerbated existing inequalities, highlighting the systemic issues that continue to plague our societies. Economic disparities, racial injustices, and unequal access to health care have become even more pronounced, reminding us of the urgent need for systemic change. The polarization that has gripped many nations has deepened, often pitting communities against each other and undermining the collective efforts needed to address these critical issues. Against this backdrop, the notion of radical self-care has taken on new dimensions. Self-care, once dismissed as a luxury or an indulgence, has become recognized as a fundamental necessity. It is through caring for ourselves that we build the resilience required to face the challenges of our time. I have affirmed in my own life that self-care is not a retreat from the world but a means to engage with it more fully, with greater clarity and strength. As we navigate the complexities of the postpandemic world, we must continue to cultivate these practices that equip us to withstand personal and collective adversities. Doing so in community reminds us that we are not alone in our struggles, and communal resilience underscores the power of solidarity in creating lasting change.

I continue to be struck daily by the duality of human experience. We have seen the best and worst of humanity — acts of selflessness and generosity juxtaposed with moments of division and despair. This duality is a reminder of our capacity for both destruction and creation, for harm and healing. It is a call to consciously choose the latter, to strive for a world where compassion and justice prevail. One of the most profound lessons from this period is the importance of adaptability. The ability to pivot, to find new ways of connecting and supporting one another, has been crucial. We have learned that resilience is not about returning to the status quo but about building something better in its place. It is about using the lessons of hardship to forge stronger, more inclusive communities. It was my hope to provide insight into this pathway when I wrote the book, and it remains my intention now. As we look to the future, there is much work to be done. The path to true equity and justice is long, and it requires the sustained efforts of individuals and communities alike. It demands that we continue to show up for ourselves and each other, that we remain committed to the principles of radical self-care. It is through these commitments that we can hope to create a world where everyone has the opportunity to thrive. The work cannot sustainably or successfully be done alone. Of this I am sure.

In this new edition of *Sit Down to Rise Up*, I invite you to revisit these themes with fresh eyes. Consider how they apply to the current moment, how they can inform your actions and interactions. How you can approach all the problems that we face individually and collectively from a place of love. Let this book be a guide and a companion on your journey toward personal and collective transformation.

Thank you for embarking on this journey with me.

With gratitude and hope,

Shelly Tygielski

Asheville, North Carolina
Summer 2024

Foreword

I first met Shelly Tygielski backstage at the Wisdom 2.0 conference in San Francisco. I was waiting to go onstage with my therapist Dan Siegel to discuss the major life transformations I was beginning to experience after two years of psychotherapy with him.

I'll never forget the rainbow-patterned sweatshirt, big long skirt (Shelly loves big long skirts), and matching rainbow hightops bounce into the backstage area with a titanic smile to match her huge head of thick black hair, the likes of which I'd only ever seen on a Barbie doll. In a sea of psychotherapists, neurophysicists, and "mindfulness experts," I was relieved to see someone wearing something so vibrant. Shelly's energy is vibrance. It grabs your attention.

What I witnessed that day was someone who lives their life in purpose. We made introductions, chitchatted, and ended up having dinner with my sister, Simone — which led to after-dinner drinks, which led to my sister and me hearing Shelly's story for the first time.

Her story and history are rich; it felt like I was speaking to someone who lives with such purpose, it's as if she is carrying the history of her ancestors with her. She spoke about meditation and radical self-care in a practical way — as a means to be a better member of society, a stronger member of your community, a lighthouse for compassion. She talked about it in a grounded, nonpatronizing way that felt modern and up-to-date. And I'm not going to pretend I didn't like that someone who taught meditation was also knocking back cocktails with me until midnight. Shelly's not only a meditation teacher, though — she's a gatherer and a provider. She inserts herself time and time again to help people when they need it the most. I remember lying awake in bed that night thinking, *What would the world be like if we all lived our lives in service to others?* and also, *God, I could be doing so much more.*

Some months later, Shelly somehow persuaded me to join her on what would be my very first meditation retreat in the woods of Barre, Massachusetts. I had personally hoped I would never find myself in such a situation, but I figured if Shelly had organized it, and *if I was serious about trying to actually be a better person*, I would definitely pick up a thing or two in my newfound quest to remain open-minded to all things that would previously have caused me to run for the hills (like meditation retreats and words like *journey* and *universe*).

The purpose of this retreat was to provide support and healing to survivors of gun violence, along with family members who had lost loved ones. I questioned whether it was even appropriate for me to be there, as I personally had no experience with gun violence and wasn't sure what my role at this retreat in the middle of the woods would be. (I have suffered loss, but not to gun violence.)

What I came to understand in those few days is what it means to show up. I didn't think I belonged at a retreat for survivors of gun violence until I realized in those few days that the very act of sitting and listening to people's stories is sometimes all that is needed. I learned that people need to be seen and listened to for proper healing to take place. I saw firsthand what it means to work together in concert and *for* each other. What it means to work as a collective. The true significance of giving, which isn't limited to giving money.

Sit Down to Rise Up is a blueprint for personal growth and effective societal contribution; it's a road map to compassion, radical self-care, what it means to be part of a community, and what it means to give and receive love. Shelly paints us a picture of how ideal the world can become if we all care for ourselves and each other a little more, and she describes what it means to lead by example and what it takes to build communities of care.

She breaks down how each of us is capable of creating small or big ripple effects if we take the time to focus on the needs and wants of our communities by coming together as a coalition in support of mutual aid, mutual respect, and mutual understanding.

She reminisces about what the world looked like when it was smaller and neighbors took care of each other in times of hardship and distress. She empowers us with the radical concept that a simple idea can become a reality and that we don't have to overwhelm ourselves with the full responsibility for changing the world. She shows us how to use the idea of "chunking" to make incremental change in our communities, step by step, with one act of love after another.

Who would you be if you lived your life in service? Who would you be if you simply committed to one act of service a day for a stranger? What would the world look like if we all had a bit more compassion? What if we knew that it only takes the kernel of an idea, some courage, and commitment to change the world by touching one person's life at a time?

This book is to be absorbed by people who want to love more. If you are reading this, you are ready to start spreading your love and about to find out how to do it.

— Chelsea Handler

2015: Shelly meditating alone in Hollywood North Beach Park, Florida. (Photo credit: Jenna Brodsky)

2019: Shelly meditating with her community in the same spot, Hollywood North Beach Park, Florida. (Photo credit: Jason Tygielski)

Introduction

I want to share the secret of life with you. It took me close to forty years to discover it, and it's probably not what you think. It has nothing to do with owning the right things or achieving certain goals or having a certain pedigree. It has nothing to do with loving people the "right" way or even achieving happiness. The secret to life is this: Show up. Show up for yourself and for others. Show up physically to create sacred spaces. Show up consistently. Show up even when others don't show up. Show up in a way that makes every person feel held. Show up in a way that makes you feel held by others.

Why? Because destiny isn't determined only by chance; it is also a choice. Consistently showing up means creating more opportunities for being in the right place at the right time, especially for opportunities that align with our values. Showing up means creating the possibility for fully experiencing life in the present moment and feeling that presence deep in our mind, body, and spirit. Ultimately, consistently showing up for ourselves lays the foundation for our life's purpose: showing up for others.

The two photos at the beginning of the introduction provide physical proof of what happens when we show up, day after day, week after week, year after year — for ourselves first, and then paving the way for others. We start with an idea, a feeling, a yearning — a *seed*. We unknowingly attract people into a magical space where they can feel safe and heard, and they, in turn, expand the edges of that space to make room for others, who in turn expand the space again to make room for more people — and so on and so on. The momentum builds, the heart swells, the movement begins and increases in strength with each day, making us more tender and gifting us with connection. Author and activist Glennon Doyle calls it "praying attention." Showing up is a form of prayer, and the space we create becomes a sanctuary. When we pray attention to the good, the bad, the ugly, the pain, the joy, and this exhilarating thing we call life, we can begin to trust that when we fully and consistently show up, things start to show up for us, too.

I began writing this book at the worst possible time — in 2020, amid the global coronavirus pandemic. The early days, when entire countries were shutting down, were a time of fear and uncertainty. So many lives were lost each day, countless people were suffering, and we were all facing a reckoning as we were forced to disconnect from the "normal" life we were used to. I imagined, as I looked around at the state of my country, what the world would look like if everyone already had all of these tools in place: an awareness of true self-care, the resources and skills to tend to ourselves, formalized coping plans, communities of care that would create a safety net and help us remove obstacles in our path to wellness, and an understanding of mutual aid as a pillar that can help to create true equity. On the other hand, more than ever before, I found myself leaning deeply into all of the resources that I had developed over the years. So as I was writing about these tools for this book, I was also intently practicing them.

As I reflect back, it seems fitting that I wrote this book during such a period of darkness and uncertainty because I am the type of person who tends to thrive in spaces where others might shrink, cave, or fall apart. I need a certain measure of chaos surrounding me in order to take the initiative. I require a good amount of pressure in order to feel compelled to charge into action; there needs to be a looming deadline for me to be at my best. It's precisely in these moments that I rise up and ask two distinct questions: What can I do about this situation/crisis/reality? And how do I come from a place of love? When I'm in this mode, others tend to take notice, congregate around me, mobilize, and become inspired to act. As you will read in these pages, I saved myself while in this mode, and in doing so, I also learned how to help others save themselves.

My hope is that this book will help you realize that you have the tools and capacity to embark on this journey, that your fractures and cracks are what make you relatable and unique, and that from these "broken" sacred spaces, a realization will emerge of the bounty that you have to offer your community and this world. Let me be clear about my own emergence: These epiphanies didn't arise overnight. They came about incrementally, sometimes painfully slowly, and they started with my willingness to become quiet and still long enough for the whispers of truth to become audible. Only after consistent practice and realizing deep meditative states did the audacity of courage arrive.

Please understand that *I am an unlikely meditator.* I have never fit the profile of someone I thought would be a meditator. But I have learned that everyone — including people like me, the outcasts and misfits, the ones who can't sit still and don't own crystals, who can't afford a closet filled with colorful yoga pants and who feel uncomfortable in yoga classes because we are overweight or still can't touch our toes, the ones who have been marginalized or are single moms and don't have a free moment to even pee without being interrupted by a child banging on the bathroom door — all of us can come together as a band of unlikelies. We can all make sure that there are no barriers to entry for anyone who wants to discover how perfectly imperfect they are, and we can convince others that the world needs their cast-off broken pieces.

This journey within led me to change the course of my well-planned life. It helped me tune in and "accidentally" create a community of other unlikely meditators, and it inspired me to quit an unfulfilling career that I invested twenty years into building. This took courage, but rooted in these tools, I connected to a deep sense of responsibility to myself and others. This process was like rushing into flames that exposed all of my flaws and fears and the many places that, from the outside, seemed broken.

Here is what I realized: Courage is cultivated through our need for connection. Connection is cultivated due to the basic human need for love. And love encourages us to be more courageous. It's a cycle, and every single one of us has this same blueprint in our DNA, but not all of us have access to the cipher required to understand this. The courage to expand our circles of influence bubbles up when we have enough self-love to first expand the circle that encompasses us.

This is a book for anyone who has at some point in their lives found themselves completely lost — standing outside of their own circle, looking in. As an adult, I once found myself in literal darkness due to total vision loss, but as I persevered in my journey, I learned there is a major difference between losing eyesight and losing vision, and that even if the eyes go blind, the mind can still see. This book is an offering, an appeal, and a road map for the type of courage that comes from true connection, the kind that helps each of us individually and paves the way for all of us to collectively flourish.

I never thought I'd write a book. I have, however, kept a regular journaling practice that began at the ripe old age of nine. This book developed from a compilation of my nearly daily personal journal entries over the last decade and from the contemplative practices that have carried me through each day, especially the days I didn't think I would live to see the end of. Every morning, I would write to myself, telling myself the words that I needed to hear and believe: *I am not broken, I am enough, I am perfectly me — cracks, faults, and all.* In 2016, I started to share some of my writings with a small group of unlikely meditators, and with their prodding and positive feedback about the impact my writing had on them, I began to share some of my journal entries on social media. Because of this connection and the feeling that I wasn't alone, I was encouraged to be vulnerable and let people see the outtakes in my life, not just the highlight reel. When I shared my struggles with my health, sadness, loneliness, and self-worth, I realized quickly that I was not alone and that my courage to speak up helped other people share their stories, too.

As you sit holding these pages and reading these words, maybe you've arrived at a place of realization that carrying on with business as usual is not the way to make it through. Perhaps you are ready to tune in to the whispers within and turn them into a roar. Perhaps every cell in your body knows that it's time to make a radical shift, that it's time to expand your circles, connect with others, and boldly rise up. Perhaps you know it is time to show up authentically and do things differently, to reimagine the impact you want to make on the world. Whatever your situation, the good news is this: You don't have to journey alone. In fact, in order to be successful on this path, you actually can't go it alone. It has to be a shared journey.

It doesn't matter what you look like, what you think of yourself, what your past is, or if you have no idea where your future is headed. This book is especially for those who don't want more cliché self-care advice — the world doesn't need another self-help book. What we need is to wake up to who we are called to be.

My premise is fairly simple: We are interconnected, so when one of us heals, we all heal. The journey to healing doesn't stop where the inner borders end and the external ones begin. The successful inner journey of *me* leads toward a collective healing of *we*. The strength of the communal *we* can then rise to the task of creating true shifts in the fabric of society — movements — by arriving at the journey to *us*. Once we understand our strengths and what makes us unique, we can lean into what we can collectively bring to our community and how we can nourish those in our circles of influence. When we understand our challenges, we know where we need to be brave enough to rely on others. When we understand the challenges of others, we know where we need to be brave enough to step up and allow others to rely on us.

Each time I sat down to write this book, I thought about all the seeds of wisdom that I have picked up throughout my life's journey. I dug deep to return to stories from my youth, from my ancestors, and from periods of my life that were scary to remember. I have divided the book into three parts that represent the three journeys of me, we, and us. Metaphorically, I envision these seeds as small points of light inside of me that, like the universe itself, will keep expanding out, growing larger and larger until they completely engulf me, then include those who are closest to me, and eventually encompass my community and the communities surrounding me. The chapters provide practical tools and techniques that you can immediately dive into and try on for size. You can return to them again and again or put them away and return to them when you need them. Each practice is portable, exportable, and free. There are tools for formal community-of-care gatherings and for organizers who are ready to move from me to we and beyond.

Our lives resemble mountain ranges — with peaks and valleys. We are constantly striving for the peaks, but the truth of the matter is that most of the strength or wisdom I've gathered throughout my life was not found on the peaks. It was found while in the bottom of the deepest valleys — rock bottom. My times at rock bottom have given me the strength to climb back up again. The hardships I've experienced have provided the impetus to shift and change. No teacher, politician, therapist, influencer, or celebrity could have done this for me. All true change — in our own lives, and in the world — emanates from within. I encourage you to embrace and learn from your valleys. Don't just climb mountains to seek wisdom, for as Rumi wrote, "The only way out, is through." Thank you for being willing to journey with me.

PART ONE

SIT DOWN

[The Inner Journey to Me]

CHAPTER ONE

Agency

He who has a why to live for can bear almost any how.

— FRIEDRICH NIETZSCHE

When I was two years old, I was kidnapped. My mother, newly arrived in this country, was trying to get her driver's license at a local DMV in Brooklyn. While she was taking her requisite eye exam, covering her eyes one at a time, I stood by her side. Somewhere between the big E and the lowest line on the chart, I was snatched by a couple.

My mother finished her exam and looked down, but I wasn't standing next to her, as she expected. Her eyes darted around the dank room, but I was nowhere in sight. Her initial confusion became full-blown hysteria, and she began running around the office, looking under desks and behind chairs. She ran outside and into the street, yelling, crying in her broken English, playing a frenzied game of charades with anyone who crossed her path: gestures for "short," "pigtails," "dress."

Our family of five had just landed in New York City from Jerusalem a few months before. It was 1979. There were no cell phones, no cameras monitoring the doors or waiting areas. The woman who conducted my mom's eye exam was among the first to understand the situation and immediately called 911. The NYPD arrived. My father was contacted at the garage where he worked as a mechanic, and after what seemed like a lifetime to my mom, he made it to the scene of the crime. As they stood holding each other in the unwelcoming waiting area, with its rusty metal seats, harsh fluorescent lighting, and linoleum flooring, the reality of the situation sank in: Their baby girl was gone. My mother thought she would never see me again.

For over an hour, their search rippled out across the immediate area, and alerts crackled across radios into the blue Plymouth Fury NYPD fleets throughout the five boroughs, when suddenly a middle-aged woman with brown hair and a plain face burst through the front door of the DMV, out of breath and sweating. She ran directly up to my mother and yelled, "I know where your daughter is!" My mother stared at her, perplexed. She didn't understand a word that was said, but the woman placed her fists on each side of her head, just above the ears, in a gesture my mother understood clearly: "pigtails."

The woman looked vaguely familiar to my mother. As it turned out, she had been sitting with my mom in the waiting area and had noticed my mother reading me a book while she waited to be called for the eye exam. Shortly after my mother and I disappeared down the fluorescent-lit corridor, the woman saw me wandering alone through the hallway. Next, she saw a tall man in orange bell-bottoms and a well-kempt afro lift me up from under my arms and carry me out the front door. At that moment, the woman had a choice — she could either run through the corridor in hopes of finding my mother and alerting her to the problem, or she could follow the man to see where he was going. For reasons I will never know, she decided to follow him outside. At this point, the man was practically running. The woman followed him down several blocks until he walked into a building. With a hope that he'd stay there, she headed back to the DMV, where by then all hell had broken loose.

Frustrated and understanding that every moment was precious, the woman grabbed my mom's hand and pulled her toward the door. "Run!" she cried, and my mother did, full of urgency, allowing this stranger to lead her around the corner and up Ocean Parkway, block after block after block. Two police officers and my father joined the chase. They all ran for several city blocks until they arrived at a brown dilapidated building: a typical Section 8–housing apartment building. When my mom recounts this story, she says there must have been at least thirty floors.

My mother, my father, the woman, and the officers rode the elevator together, got off on each floor, and ran up and down the hallways looking for yours truly. My mom used the "pigtails" gesture to communicate with anyone she encountered among the dreary halls. The good Samaritan who led my mom to this place asked everyone for help. Yet I was nowhere to be found, and my mother became more and more hopeless.

On the twenty-fourth floor, my exhausted mother, head drooped, eyes swollen, legs tired, and heart heavy, looked up as the doors of the elevator slid open. Right in front of the elevator stood a heavy-set woman wearing a floral house dress with rollers in her hair. I was in her arms.

As if nothing was out of the ordinary, I was hugging this

woman tightly around her neck and playing with the pink rollers wobbling around her head. "Shelly!!!" my mom cried out. When I heard my name and saw my mother, I instinctively leaped from the woman and into my mother's waiting arms. She clung to me tightly in the elevator, then broke down — the love, anger, and relief all pouring out at once.

"Why are you crying, Eema?" I innocently asked my mother. I turned around; the woman who had held me was being dragged away from the elevator and further into the hallway by the police. "Look, Eema, I made a new friend." As the elevator doors closed, I enthusiastically waved goodbye to my new "friend." My mother and the angel who had guided her to me sobbed uncontrollably and hugged me the whole way back down to the lobby. All the while, I was joyfully oblivious to the fact that I had ever been lost at all. The universe, working its magic, had somehow sent that woman to the waiting room at the Brooklyn DMV, ensuring that I would have the opportunity to live this version of my life and tell you this story.

But this is not really *my* story. This is a story about a good Samaritan, a person who, aware of her own agency, followed her gut and was bold and brave enough to do what she thought was right and kind. She didn't hesitate or think about what could possibly happen to her by following that man; I can only assume that my safety and well-being were more important to her. This is the story of a stranger who saved my life or at the very least prevented the path of my life from taking a very different course.

Throughout my childhood, this event was recounted at family gatherings, dinner parties, and life events. Those who had never heard it before naturally reacted with shock and horror, but in ways that became expected, such as expressing empathy for my mother — "That must have been so scary! Thank God you found her!" — and telling me I needed to remember how lucky I was to have ever been found.

The truth is, every single time I heard this story replayed, I did not think about how fortunate I was to be "saved." I thought about the woman who found me and what it would take for me to have the same courage to stand up for what is right and for people who have no ability to stand up for themselves. What would I be willing to risk for someone I didn't know? This stranger planted that seed within me, one that I have carried with me ever since.

For a large majority of my life, I thought there was a prerequisite for this type of courage. My family didn't really stay in touch with the woman, and so I never got to meet her and don't even know her name. In my mind I painted her out to be a full-fledged superhero, like Wonder Woman. I was certain that I couldn't possibly make a similar positive impact on the world because I hadn't reached whatever she had reached: a specific destination as a fully matured and completely intact agent of change. I felt broken, and so for a large majority of my life, I waited to reach that proverbial starting line because I believed that broken people can't help fix other broken people. People who need fixing can't have this kind of agency, they don't have the right or even the ability to access it, and certainly nobody would want them to have that responsibility.

Only later in my life — after a traumatic moment of truth that left me feeling beyond broken, shattered — did I recognize that I had the whole thing wrong: We are all broken. Others have the pieces that I am missing, and I have the shards that others need to fill in their cracks. I developed a new premise: You, I, and everyone are already whole, just as we are. There is nothing to fix. Real growth and healing aren't about finding what doesn't exist, but about expanding what already does.

I eventually learned that not only am I capable of being a good Samaritan like the one who saved me, but I actually have an inherent responsibility to try to be one. This sense of duty was not instilled in me later in life — no. It was, in fact, something that I was born with — that we are each born with: a sense of agency, *a seed of agency* that can sometimes be revealed in only the harshest situations. I learned that the best people to help those who are "broken" are, in fact, those who recognize their own brokenness. The Sufi poet Rumi wrote that "the wound is the place where the light enters you." I believe these wounds, the cracks, are how our light also escapes into the world and helps to heal others.

While waiting in a doctor's office, I once read a magazine article about the jack pine, which tends to blend in with its surroundings. I'm no arborist, but I found myself engrossed by this fascinating species. Most of the time, the jack pine fools us into thinking it's just another tree, but it does some pretty remarkable things. When hot, fast-moving fires are frequent, this particular species of pine develops very thick, hard cones that are literally glued shut with a strong resin.

These serotinous cones can hang on the tree or lie on the forest floor for *years*, long after the enclosed seeds mature. Some of these seeds can remain buried in the soil for decades — totally in the dark. Only when a raging fire sweeps through, melting the resin, do these heat-dependent cones finally open up, releasing seeds that are then distributed by wind, animal transport, and gravity, sowing the souls of a future forest, a new day, a better day.

Much to the dismay of the other folks in the waiting room, I sat there reading and saying emphatically, "Yes! Mmm-hmm." You see, you and I, *we are the jack pine* in any of its forms — sometimes we are the tree, and sometimes we are the cone lying dormant on the forest floor. Some of us are the seeds buried deep in the Earth, unable to discern that there is even the possibility of a new day. When fire comes, it may seem like it will consume all the trees, and the forest will be destroyed and all will be lost. We don't realize the transformative power of the fire, which paves the way for each of us to rise again and affirm that all is not lost.

Throughout my life, I have vacillated between feeling like I was on fire trying to save myself or actively running into the flames trying to save someone else. In either case, I now know that the flames help reveal something incredibly important in me by cracking me wide open. The seeds of agency are always there. We just have to dig through the layers to get to them; we need to believe that we are worthy of being an agent of change. We have to reclaim the agency that has been our God-given right since the day we were born, and then we have to help others reclaim theirs.

The Meaning of Agency

Before getting too deep into this forest, I want to address what it means to have agency. In a general sense, when I say that someone "has agency," I mean they are an independent and self-governing person, that they are capable of voluntarily analyzing their knowledge, setting intentions or goals, making plans, and acting on them. In the simplest terms, this can be synonymous with free will. In the context of the social construct of modern Western civilization, agency means people recognize how their choices born from this free will affect other people. It means that they have the ability to be reflective, have awareness, and be introspective about their actions. A person who has agency has control over their thoughts and actions, they take responsibility for the consequences of their

SIT DOWN: The Inner Journey to Me

actions, and they consistently lean into opportunities to expand their capacity to grow and have positive impacts, both individually and collaboratively. In general, mentally healthy individuals have a greater sense of agency, even amid a state of chaos or tragedy.

Each one of us is born with free will, with agency. But self-awareness of having agency only occurs as we mature. We *always* have agency from the day we are born, but we might not recognize our autonomy until we reach a specific age or experience a major life event. It can take longer for some than others to have a "sense" of agency. *Agency and a sense of agency are two different things.*

Sociologists define agency as an expression of individual power, even within a defined or perceived social structure. To have a sense of agency means that in spite of the social structure (or structures) a person identifies with, they can rise up and assert themselves outside of those constructs, becoming an agent for change that benefits the social structure, and sometimes even benefits themselves and the greater good. For example, Rosa Parks had a sense of agency when she decided not to give up that seat on the bus; the students at Marjory Stoneman Douglas High School in Parkland, Florida, had a sense of agency after the mass shooting that took seventeen lives in their community; and I and hundreds of volunteers had a sense of agency when the Covid-19 pandemic hit in 2020 and we started Pandemic of Love, the global mutual-aid organization that has helped millions of people across the world. The point is that agency is associated with a choice that requires action and has a certain goal or value in mind, one that extends beyond the self.

In order to improve our ability to take action, to increase our influence, and to exert control over our own lives, we need to develop our sense of agency. If we want others to be able to depend on us, we need to cultivate it. With it we can develop into stable, resilient, and flexible individuals. Without it, we lose our sense of control over our own lives. We may even come to believe that we don't have the power to influence our own thoughts, let alone our actions. We may resign ourselves to the idea that we have no power over the trajectory of our lives. And if we believe we have no power over that, then we assuredly cannot show up to help others with the trajectory of their lives, nor for that matter can we affect the trajectory of the world.

Ask yourself this: *At this very moment, do you believe that you have agency over your own life?*

The answer I most frequently get when I pose this question to others is: "It depends on what area of my life we are talking about." Most people believe that they have control only over certain aspects of their lives. But adhering to certain societal structures like practicing a certain religion or following certain laws or conforming to cultural standards is — except in very radical, extreme circumstances — a choice. Even in the most extreme cases, one could argue that we still retain agency over whether we want to relinquish the one thing that can never be taken away from us — *the way we mentally choose to respond to something.*

I am not saying that life is not hard or that we can always do whatever we want. Sometimes our choices are limited because the cards life has dealt us are traumatic, downright unfair, and sometimes even unbearable. Yet in spite of even the harshest circumstances, we can use our agency to identify purpose, meaning, and a will to live, to survive and even thrive. While I was an undergraduate in college, I read the work of Dr. Viktor Frankl, an Austrian Jew who was the only member of his family to survive the Holocaust. Frankl spent time in four different concentration camps, including Auschwitz. As required reading in an introductory philosophy course, we were assigned Frankl's 1946 book *Man's Search for Meaning*, in which he wrote about his experiences. While enduring the atrocities of each day, he was motivated to continue to live by "a will to meaning" — essentially, the aspiration to find meaning in his remaining life. I distinctly remember my professor reading this sentence out loud while standing in front of our classroom. I underlined it in my book fervently:

"Everything can be taken from a man but one thing: the last of the human freedoms — to choose one's attitude in any given set of circumstances."

In Frankl's case, he retained a sense of agency over his inner world despite what was happening in the world around him. Of course, heated debate ensued in the classroom, stoked by our professor. Some asked what was the point of even having meaning, or trying to be unbreakable or have strong moral character, when as a prisoner in the atrocious concentration camps you knew you would probably perish. Clearly, the prisoners knew the odds were not in their favor. Our professor explained that this assumed that the will to live was about survival. Instead, Frankl was saying this is a choice a person makes about how to live in each moment, that the only thing individuals cannot be robbed of is the free will, the agency, to make that choice.

In my tattered copy of Frankl's book from my sophomore year, I also double underlined the following sentence: "In accepting this challenge to suffer bravely, life has a meaning up to the last moment, and it retains this meaning literally to the end. In other words, life's meaning is an unconditional one, for it even includes the potential meaning of unavoidable suffering."

Frankl founded and developed a form of psychotherapy called logotherapy — *logos* being the Greek word for meaning — which posits that our lives retain meaning up until our final moments, in terrible and normal circumstances alike. The difference in each moment is relative for each person — and it obviously relates to their circumstances, such as whether they are a prisoner in a concentration camp or living in a peaceful country during prosperous times. Yet all individuals have the option to never lose agency over their inner world, in the here and now.

Like the cone of a jack pine that lies dormant for years and whose seeds are buried for decades, our inner world may feel inaccessible at one point or another in our lives. We may feel like we have no control, no choice, no agency, but it is worth considering during these dark periods that sometimes the tragedy, the major challenge, the hardship is actually the onset of a blazing fire, and that amid the flames, we have an opportunity. We are at a crossroads, and we can choose being bitter or getting better. At these critical moments, we can tap into our sense of agency and actively choose to get and do better, to connect with our inner world even as flames rage around us. This inner connection has the potential to manifest in the outer world in beautiful, contributory ways.

Using Agency to Find Meaning

As human beings, acceptance of agency helps us overcome fear and gain a sense of ownership, without which we cannot act. Acting on anything requires formulating the thought first, and without this acknowledgment of agency over our thoughts, we can't progress to accessing our autonomy or working toward finding our purpose. Of course, accepting that we always have agency over our thoughts and actually living this way are two different things. Yet being able to do this in any circumstance begins with the desire to embark on this inner work. The awakening of this desire can arrive at any moment, regardless of what stage of life we are in — it may happen in good times, when we experience ourselves as independent, free-thinking human beings with many choices, or it may arise in bad times, when we realize that all we can control is our minds, since we can't control or change what is happening in the world around us.

Sociology professor Jim Côté at the University of Western Ontario in Canada has been studying what he calls "agentic personality" for years. He defines this term as a composition of four overlapping personality traits: a person's sense of resilience, their sense of meaning or purpose, their sense of worth or self-esteem, and their sense of control over the things that occur in their life. Côté says people with agentic personalities believe in their own abilities and capabilities to live a fulfilling life, they are goal oriented and have a sense of direction in their lives, they can bounce back from a setback or failure, and they understand the concept of cause and effect when it comes to the decisions they make in their lives.

Here is where the rubber meets the road: In order to practically cultivate a sense of agency, or an agentic personality, we need to look at the big picture and also at the up-close, microscopic version. Having a sense of agency day to day means identifying your values and making sure that you are always (or as much as possible!) acting in integrity with them. What do you stand for? What do you believe about the world and your place in it? How do you feel about yourself? Would any of those things change if your situation changed for the worse? If you answer no to the last question, then you are well on your way to living a life of meaning that is aligned with your values. If you think that any of the things you believe would shift — what you stand for, the way you feel about the world, your place in it, your feelings about

22

yourself — as a result of the world around you changing, then you haven't claimed your sense of agency in the fullest sense.

Another question that helps in the search for meaning is this: What inspires you to wake up in the morning? To live life on purpose? To know that you are walking on the right path regardless of any obstacles that may be present on the journey before you? I've heard it said that purpose and meaning can be defined when three things align: our values, our core competencies, and our passions. But that really isn't the whole picture at all. Identifying the intersection of those three areas is only part of the story. Having a sense of agency and meaning in life is all about one thing, and one thing only: giving. Striving for abstract things like success, happiness, or inner peace is counterintuitive. It's like telling a person who is agitated to calm down. Never in the history of "calm down" has saying those two words ever calmed anybody down.

"Don't aim at success," wrote Frankl. "The more you aim at it and make it a target, the more you are going to miss it. For success, like happiness, cannot be pursued; it must ensue, and it only does so as the unintended side effect of one's personal dedication to a cause greater than oneself or as the by-product of one's surrender to a person other than oneself." To boil this down: If you want to be more successful, help make other people successful; if you want to lead a happier and more joyful life, bring happiness and joy to others; if you want more love, love others more.

Our life's meaning and sense of agency come together when our values are backed by our core competencies in a passionate way *and* we use the outcome of this in service of others. Here are two Venn diagrams that visualize the difference between these concepts. Some say that meaning arises when three aspects intersect, like this:

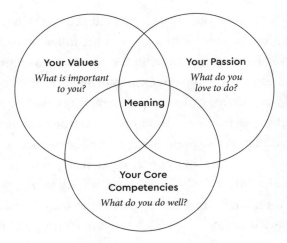

I would say — and I think Frankl might agree — that all of this occurs within a larger context of service:

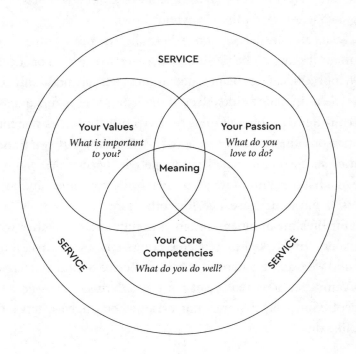

Now, before you grab a pen and paper and start listing your values, your passions, and your core competencies in order to define what holds the most meaning for you, let's zoom out a little further, with an even wider lens. Ask yourself: Do you *already* feel worthy and good enough to embark on this investigation or pursuit of agency?

Forgo the Guru, Become the Yuru

Every time I teach meditation or speak to a crowd, I tell everyone to forgo the guru and find the "yuru" — the guru within. We need to believe that we are our own guru. We all spend a lifetime climbing the proverbial mountain with an expectation that we'll find a wise person at the top who will tell us the meaning of life. This person doesn't exist, I promise. The ability to thrive, love, be happy, and feel fulfilled comes from within. Every single bit of it. It comes from the realization that we have been bestowed with the gift of agency to choose how and when to cultivate it in ourselves. If we allow external factors to control our destiny, we will spend a lifetime climbing that mountain, and when we finally reach the pinnacle, the old person staring back will be our own reflection. All we will find is a mirror. And when we are standing before it, will we be fulfilled or disappointed with what we find?

What I eventually learned through the trial and error of living is that the feeling of inner strength and fulfillment can be enough for us to move mountains. For the most part, we all have the desire to do and be great. It's just a matter of having the agency and stamina to find the right pieces to put together to make it happen. Part of that discovery process is being able to overcome the low states of energy that hold us back from finding our inner happiness and confidence. When we feel refreshed, vibrant, and able to make the right choices for ourselves, the right actions and results follow.

When I was growing up, at least up until my son was born, I viewed the sources of happiness and fulfillment in my life as events that were few and far between. I believed that, for the most part, I had little control over them. I'd have some good days here and there, but they were mostly based on what didn't go wrong at work, at home, in my relationships, or with my health. This attitude certainly took a toll on my self-esteem and sense of worth.

In contrast, it was also hard to be great when I didn't feel great. Events that I had no control over ruled my thoughts, feelings, and actions. I felt powerless over the circumstances of my own life, and therefore I couldn't even fathom how to relate to — let alone show up for — what was happening in the world at large. When someone would ask how I was doing, my reply was always preceded by a long and drawn-out sigh. Then one day, the levee broke. I refilled my own well, drop by drop, restored my own faith in myself, and realized that I was my best guru and that I always had the agency to do something — I just didn't have the strength to do it. It wasn't that something had to give; it was someone — and that someone was me. All the things that I once considered problems and issues became symptoms of my own decisions and efforts. By becoming aware of the symptoms, I knew I had the ability to treat the root causes.

Frankl based his logotherapy practice on three pillars: the notion that each person has a healthy inner core; that our primary focus should be to help others recognize the existence of this inner core and provide them with the tools to access it; and that life can promise us purpose and meaning but it cannot guarantee that we will be happy and fulfilled. Know this: The odds of reaching a level of relative happiness and fulfillment favor those with a defined purpose and meaning.

CHAPTER TWO

Good Is Good Enough

*When you are trying to motivate yourself, appreciate the fact
that you're even thinking about making a change.
And as you move forward, allow yourself to be good enough.*

— ALICE DOMAR

I am one generation removed from an illiterate woman who
lived on a mountaintop in Baghdad. My grandmother, an observant Sephardic Jewish woman, wore only modest dresses,
covered her hair, and was by all accounts a subservient wife and
mother. Her role as caretaker to her children and husband was
clear. She was so dutiful, in fact, that when my grandfather decided to marry another woman, which was a common practice at
that time period and in her country, her opinion or desires were
not taken into consideration, and she instead stayed put to help
accommodate the "new" wife. As a result, my grandmother, whom

we affectionately called "Toto" — which means "grandmother" in her native tongue — became a second-class citizen in her own home, continuing to bear children to her husband and striving to live harmoniously with her new sister-wife. Growing up, visiting Israel, I accepted this as a normal family configuration, and it was only when I shared this with my American friends back home and experienced their jarring reactions that I realized there was nothing normal about it. I became ashamed of this part of my life, worrying that it would somehow define what people thought about me. So I hid that part of me away from my American friends.

I couldn't speak to my grandmother very well. She spoke a dialect of Aramaic native to Iraqi Kurds and some Arabic, and I was raised speaking Hebrew and English. Instead, I communicated with her through my heart. She was a soft-spoken, quiet woman who always had her long hair in two neat braids and covered with a handkerchief or shawl. She wore long dresses in dark colors that looked like housecoats with subtle patterns of flowers. She always smelled like fresh pita bread or fried dough, with a hint of some spice like coriander, turmeric, or cumin — except on Friday nights, when I would watch her light the Shabbat candles and hug her waist. Then she would smell like a fresh bar of soap. It was the smell of a hard-earned reward given to a woman who spent six straight days and nights either in the kitchen or hand-washing and hanging laundry on a clothesline. Shabbat — the Jewish Sabbath — started every Friday evening at sundown and was a full day of rest. After the Shabbat candles were ceremoniously lit, and while we waited for the men and boys to return from synagogue, I would watch her do something very rare — sit down and do nothing. In those brief moments, she finally seemed at peace. I would often crawl into her lap while she was sitting on the couch watching a Turkish soap opera on one of the two television stations available at the time in Israel, or when she was on a bench on my uncle's balcony constructed of Jerusalem limestone in their old, historic neighborhood. When I was younger, my grandmother's lap seemed like the most serene place I could be — a sanctuary — but as I grew older, long after she passed (which happened when I was in the third grade), I reflected back and understood that I confused her sadness for serenity. I couldn't fully communicate with my grandmother because I didn't know how to speak the language of loss yet.

My mother, born in 1947, is one of seventeen children, eight from my grandmother Toto and nine half-siblings from my grandfather's "other" wife, whose name was Hallo (pronounced "hollow") and whom I also grew to love. When my mom was just two years old, in 1949, her family — the entire Biri clan — was airlifted from Iraq to Israel in the middle of the night, along with the majority of Iraqi Jews living in the country at the time. Following the 1947 UN Partition Plan for Palestine and after Israeli independence in 1948, a wave of anti-Semitism hit Iraq. All Jews working in the government were removed from their positions, and hundreds were arrested on dubious charges of being Zionists or Communists. Within days of the first successful airlift of 150 Jews from Iraq to Israel, over thirty thousand Iraqi Jews registered to leave within fifteen days. "One suitcase per family" was the rule. If Iraqi Jews chose to stay or could not leave within fifteen days, they were offered no protections and were considered stateless refugees.

My grandfather, David, arrived in the newly formed country of Israel in 1949 with that one suitcase, seventeen children, two wives, and a few grandchildren. While this lifestyle was commonplace in Iraq, it was looked down upon, even taboo, when they arrived in Israel, which was still comprised of a majority of literate, Eastern and Western European Jews — those who had survived the Holocaust and other pogroms or had made their way to Israel long before statehood to help build a nation. Since they were refugees with very little money, my grandfather decided, in order to fit in, that the family had to separate. With the help of a brother who had emigrated to Jerusalem years before, he found an apartment to live in with his "other" wife and kids, and my grandmother Toto went to live with her youngest, unmarried children (which included my toddler-aged mother) in the new home of her oldest son, who was already married and had children of his own.

My mother and I have often talked about how, while she felt truly loved and cared for by her mother and elder siblings, she still felt a sense of unworthiness of her father's affection. All the daughters in the family experienced this, but it became more prominent for her because of this separation. When it came to obtaining his affection or attention, she had three strikes going against her. First, she was born a girl. In that time, in that place, to that family, being born a girl generally meant that your lot in life was predetermined. Had she been born in a different slot in the pecking order, my mother, like her sisters before her, would likely have been married off as early as age twelve, and "love" would not have been a prerequisite for her nuptials.

Second, my mother grew up not living with her father. He didn't get to know her personality or enjoy her clever and curious nature. She would see him on occasions like the Sabbath, Jewish holidays, and family celebrations. It didn't matter to him that my mother was the first of his daughters to study beyond primary school because she was living in a modernized country that valued the education of women, nor that she learned how to read and write, or that she dreamed of something greater than finding someone willing to marry her.

Third, my mother grew up with a dual narrative. This was the golden age of pioneers building the new Jewish state, a time when strong Israeli women were enlisting in the resistance and staking their claim in society. My mother found herself commingling with girls at school from Eastern European, secular Jewish households whose parents were scholars and professionals and who were planning on getting an education themselves or enlisting in the military after high school. My mother listened to records by Elvis Presley and Ricky Nelson, she ironed her hair and set it into a beehive updo, and she plucked her eyebrows and wore pencil skirts. She was part of the new culture anchored to an old, outdated order. Beyond her household and family, my mother was free to explore who she wanted to be; however, each day she would return to the family narrative — a confining box of values and standards she adhered to in order to uphold her "good Jewish girl" reputation. After all, her family's honor was always at stake, and absolutely nothing was more important than that.

My mother once told me this story: One evening as a teenager she made plans to meet her friends for an evening out. It was a special night in her eyes, and she planned to dress for the occasion. My mom slipped into a slim-fitting pencil skirt that fell just below her knees and put on a matching sleeveless top. She carefully applied her makeup and spent hours crafting her hair into the perfect updo. As she was preparing to leave the house, excited to meet her friends, she was surprised to find her father standing on the front porch. He'd come to visit his eldest son. He took one look at her, grunted with disgust, and told her she was dressed like a prostitute, bringing shame to the family. My mother's face turned red, tears started to stream down her face, and she ran back to her room with no more plans to go anywhere that night.

I fully believe that my mother's deep-seated need for her father's love and approval, which never came, contributed to her lack of self-esteem as an adult. This void was magnified later in life when she arrived as the dutiful wife, silently kicking and screaming, to America — a country where she knew nobody, didn't speak the language, and had no transferable job skills. She resented being brought to this country in every way. In Israel, she was an independent woman: She met and decided on her own to marry my father — and for love! She had a driver's license and drove her own car, and she was a working woman who had a prized job at the Ministry of Interior, where she was well-liked and steadily climbing the ranks. She was slowly coming into her own womanhood, becoming self-assured and confident. Then, like her mother before her, she was forced to accept decisions about her life made by someone else and stripped from the only place she had ever known. Only in this case, she wasn't seeking political asylum; her husband, my father, was seeking adventure, opportunity, and riches. One day she was nestled among the cozy streets of Jerusalem with her entire extended family close by as a web of support; the next she was trying to find her way around the bustling streets of New York City, where she didn't know a living soul.

Unlike many immigrants, my mother didn't long to come to America. She had no "American dreams" or yearning to cross the Atlantic. But she didn't have a choice because in spite of her "independence," she still had an anchor tying her down: family honor. Women in my family were not raised to be strong and empowered. They were raised to be nurturing, kind, and submissive.

They were taught early on to do as they were told and to accept that suffering was an inevitable part of their lives. When my father randomly announced that he had found a job in New York and that we were moving, I imagine that an internal battle ensued within my mother: Her strong-willed, confident side said, "No way!" but the good girl who didn't want to disappoint her family knew that "a dutiful wife follows her husband." My mother's subservient side won, and I truly believe that the move was so traumatic for her that she regressed to a state of insecurity. And so, in 1979, my mother arrived at the shores of New York with crushed dreams, three children under the age of twelve, and suitcases filled with sadness, loss, and resentment.

The Traits That Are Passed Down

I am convinced that this feeling of unworthiness and self-doubt, the persistent feeling of less-than, must have been passed down from my grandmother to my mother and then to me. I am the product of intergenerational trauma. I can't explain it any other way. While genetics only play a part in determining who we become — environment, surroundings, and upbringing play large roles as well — I am certain that I was born with that "unworthy" gene because, for as long as I can remember, I have *always* felt like I was inadequate — whether I was in the United States or back in Israel, where I, too, was born. I didn't belong anywhere. When I was in the United States, I wasn't American enough, and when I was in Israel, I wasn't Israeli enough. Growing up in secular America, I was "too Jewish," but visiting Israel, I felt like I was "not Jewish enough." I didn't look like my friends; I didn't have the same traditions, eat the same foods, or speak the same language at home. For most of my life, my achievements were motivated by an unquenchable need for approval and an exhaustive drive for praise from others, from my family and friends, from *anyone*. This way of existence left me always feeling like nothing I ever did was good enough and that I always had to go above and beyond what was expected of me to try and prove my worth to others. I wanted to be validated by someone, anyone. I desperately wanted to know that I belonged. To something. To somewhere. To anything.

Like my grandmother and my mother before me, I spent almost every day of a large portion of my life meticulously piecing together the evidence that I did not deserve to be loved, that I would never be able to live up to my potential, and that everyone's conclusion would affirm that I was a nobody. The voice of my inner critic was loud and persistent, and it completely dismantled my self-esteem and sense of worth. I became a reflection of all the people I believed didn't love me and could never love me or even like me. That noise drowned out the voices of the people who did.

My grandmother's path was dictated by the circumstances of her time, of course, but also by her inability to understand that she was worthy of something better. My mother's path was dictated by her fear of disappointing her family and her lack of confidence. My path was dictated by my desire to belong and feel validated. My saving grace was that, one day, I was fortunate enough to understand something my maternal ancestors did not — that I had the agency to do something about my crippling way of showing up in the world. I was finally able to recognize that my obsession with being perceived as perfect was just a wrapper for my need to show other people that I deserved to be loved.

Validation Is for Parking, Not Humans

Here is what I finally learned through hard and painful lessons: Validation is for parking, not humans. The need for approval doesn't only kill one's freedom; it stunts growth. It turns us into our own worst enemies, and our default mode becomes being terrible to ourselves. We compare ourselves to others, and our need for approval becomes insatiable because we cannot stand just being "good." For some, in order to feel worthy, they have to be the best, feel loved by all, and feel praised. For others, they lack the confidence to grasp our God-given right to free will; they dread the possibility of making the wrong choices, so instead they actively make none. But not choosing is in itself a choice.

The only thing that is guaranteed when we live our lives to please others is that we will eventually disappoint them and that we will *always* disappoint ourselves. And the only thing that is guaranteed when striving for perfection is that we will fall short of that unrealistic goal. One of the biggest causes for our self-loathing is the need to be perfect — by our own standards or by those of others. Before we can embark on any inner work or experience true growth, we must unshackle ourselves from the narratives that are holding us back. And if we are ever going to show up for ourselves authentically (or for others), we need to have the courage to remind ourselves that *good is good enough* and that *good enough is better than perfect.*

The sum total of the raw components that we are made of — the good, the bad, and the ugly, all that makes us what we are and who we are — is a good enough place for us to start getting better and being better. The fundamental building blocks that we are made of are always — and have always been — a good enough place to work from. We are already good enough, and we must believe that each of our components provides what we need in order to build a fulfilling life. First, we must realize that only we have the agency to do so. So many people are stuck in this "failure to launch" mode, paralyzed as they wait until their life has a better ratio and possesses more good than bad, or more bad than ugly, so to speak. This is a fallacy. In every step of my journey, I have learned that we need nothing more than what we have now.

What if we all believed that our personal starting line is our current version of ourselves, including any internal fractures? What if we accepted that a battle will always occur within us because we are made up of contradicting thoughts, emotions, attitudes, beliefs, and characteristics? We have the capacity to be both afraid *and* courageous, trusting *and* suspicious, joyful *and* sad. To me, the notion that we are born with everything we need is incredibly comforting because it means we already hold the fundamental building blocks to not only survive but thrive. It means that what we possess is enough.

When I was little, I remember watching reruns of astronomer Carl Sagan's *Cosmos* on PBS. Even if I couldn't understand much of what he explained, the one thing that has stuck with me is the idea that, because energy cannot be created or destroyed, only transformed, we are all made of stars. We are all part of a magical congregation of particles and light twirling together. Therefore, as we each sit on the front lines of our ancestral lineage, fraught with the residue of unfinished business, I imagine that some of the particles that we are made of — beyond the genetic material — embody the energy of our mothers and fathers, and our grandmothers and great-grandfathers, and so on. We have the ability to transform that energy, and each generation has the same potential. We are the energy that can heal the old wounds of our ancestors and dictate what our future descendants will inherit.

We can relinquish conditioned beliefs, generational strife and hatred, and the fear and pain that have been passed on from one wick to the next, like one candle lighting another. We are the ones who can choose to extinguish the flame and redirect that energy elsewhere in other ways. We can nullify the unspoken family agreements to keep the flame going, not only because we have a sense of agency, but because we feel worthy of that power. We are good enough now.

We can harness and redirect the energy for future generations because the future depends directly on the energy we put out in this lifetime, in this physical body. We have free will and can choose: Do we view this responsibility as a burden or as a gift, an opportunity to contribute to those we will never meet or know? We can recalibrate energy, not just for those who will come after us but to provide a collective healing for those who came before us. Even those who merely witness these efforts will gain access to possibilities that were not seized by our ancestors. If we find ourselves still hard-pressed to believe at times that we are worthy, we can take comfort that those who come after us surely will. They will build upon our work, just as we are building upon our ancestors' toil. We don't need to be perfect. That pressure is off because it has never been any individual's responsibility to be perfect. If, collectively, we can be satisfied with good enough and do our best, we will build something exquisite out of our flaws.

Pause for a moment and reflect on how often people's judgments, perceptions, and assumptions about others are off the mark. Then think about how each one of us is also an "other" from someone else's perspective. I remember once sitting in horrendous rush-hour gridlock on the highway after picking up my meditation teacher and friend Sharon Salzberg from the airport. I audibly complained about the traffic, and Sharon quickly responded: "We are the traffic, too." A friend of Sharon's once said this to her, and now whenever I am miserably sitting in bumper-to-bumper traffic, I remind myself that "I am the traffic" to everyone else. So, too, whenever I am spiraling into the vortex of "I am not good enough," I remind myself that, by the same perfectionist standards, neither is anyone else. This prompts me to put aside this comparative thinking and remember that we are all good enough. We are all equally the traffic. We can lose sight of this, and mistakenly see everyone *else* as the traffic, or only ourselves as not good enough, but it's all relative depending on where we sit. The encouraging news is that we have the capacity to learn and choose a new way of thinking — about ourselves, others, and the world.

The first step is recognizing that adopting a new way of thinking and being is a remodeling project, not a new construction project. We don't build from the ground up. Rather, we take the personal foundation that already exists, that is already good enough, then *de*construct it in order to *re*construct it in a better way. Here is how I deconstructed my own narratives and examined my own ways of thinking. It's an account of how my pen became a pickax and then, eventually, a hammer.

Deconstructing Ourselves

For decades — starting in the fifth grade — I kept an (almost) daily journal of the events and sometimes the emotions of each day. There is only a gap of about seven years when I fell away from this practice, which coincided with my first marriage, motherhood, and my divorce. I probably have close to a hundred journals of all colors and sizes sitting in boxes in storage. But as an adult, as part of my quest for self-worth and healing, I aimed to do something different with the fresh, new, bright red journal I picked up one day on the large, wooden table at the front entrance of a bookstore. This was not a journal for a daily dump. This was a journal for deconstruction. My goal was to sit down with a pen and paper and actually write down all of the narratives that had contributed to the walls I had built over time — the walls that needed to come down. Each day, as I sat with the journal closed before me, pen in hand, I reminded myself, often multiple times throughout the day, that the walls were going to come down incrementally — one spoonful of plaster at a time, à la the escape from prison in the movie *The Shawshank Redemption*. I wasn't going to use my usual over-the-top wrecking-ball style for this job. I wanted to manage my expectations and tell myself that one spoonful a day was good enough.

The questions that I sat down to try and answer were pretty straightforward and simple, and yet the answers only got clearer and more articulate after many passes. Why? Because our habitual narratives are so strong. Our mental blocks are like seemingly impermeable walls. Only upon closer examination are they revealed to be, in fact, porous. To use another analogy, we must sift through our clouded thoughts, straining the unwanted, unhelpful material, to get to clear ones. Muddy waters don't become clear on the first pass. Each morning, after reminding myself of all of this, I would pause, open to a blank page, and respond to the following prompts:

→ What must I do to consider myself a success?

I have to be perfect. I have to be better than others or the best relative to others. I need to feel validated. I need to feel worthy of praise.

→ Where does this belief come from?

I grew up with a father that had erratic mood swings and I thought that I could "fix" whatever stress or unhappiness others in my household were feeling by being perfect and by going above and beyond.

→ Is this belief limiting? Is this belief true?

yes. The belief limits me from being authentic because I do things to first please others, gain their favor or praise. The belief is not true but it <u>still feels real</u>. The belief is also physically exhausting me.

→ What do I physically feel in response to this belief?

Panic attacks, massive anxiety, the inability to enjoy the moment or the aftermath of success. The inability to enjoy the journey to success. I feel sick to my stomach.

→ What actions do I take as a result of this belief?

I take on more than I can handle or that any person should handle. I go over the top to make sure things are perfect. I compromise my own health, my mental and physical well being for others and to achieve a result. I am unable to be or feel content.

→ What are the consequences of this belief?
    I am rewarded by society for my hard
work and productivity. I am recognized,
I am rewarded with promotions or accolades
and honors. I am never able to feel
satisfied. I am never able to feel worthy.
I am never able to feel validated for my
efforts.

For several weeks, day after day, I responded to these prompts. Here is what I learned about myself: In order to feel successful, I have to be perfect, or at the very least "the best" relative to others. I need to know more facts and figures than my colleagues or friends in order to feel valued, loved, and validated. The first instance that I can recall feeling this way was in kindergarten, when I pretended to be able to read a book that was far too advanced for the entire class. I was four years old and craved this validation from others. Why? Because I grew up with the narrative that whatever stress and unhappiness existed in our household was something that I could "fix" by being cute, bringing home good grades, and winning awards or recognitions. This belief spilled over into my friendships and relationships.

If my parents were not on speaking terms as we sat down for our evening supper, then I would whip out an A+ paper or talk about how I won the lead in the new school musical. Had a teacher assigned a project that was supposed to be done on regular poster board? I would accompany it with a diorama, make it three-dimensional, and create an over-the-top presentation when unveiling this in front of my classmates. What did I do when a girl in one of my seventh-grade classes didn't particularly like me (or at least I decided she didn't)? I gave her my coveted New Kids on the Block concert ticket to get her to like me, and then I lied to my father, telling him the ticket was stolen so he would buy me another one. In eleventh grade, what happened when I realized that I would not be valedictorian and that I was, in fact, not the "smartest" person in the school (as measured by grade-point averages)? I applied for early entrance to attend university the following year, in lieu of completing or competing in my senior year of high school.

You get the drift.

Of course, from the very first day I sat down to write in my journal and answer these prompts, I knew that these beliefs were not true and that they were limiting. But here's the thing: Just because something isn't true doesn't mean it still can't be very real. It was real when it caused me to have crippling anxiety attacks as I would get ready in the mornings before heading out to tackle the day. It was real before a big event — when I would stress out to the point of complete panic, orchestrating every minute detail to ensure perfection and forgetting to enjoy myself in the process. It was real when I would spend many nights working on group projects by myself because I did not trust anyone else's input. It surely was real when I could not accept anyone's compliments, but instead focused on the one negative comment or the one thing that went wrong, incessantly comparing myself to everyone else.

In my journal, I also took note of my physical responses during "high-performance" times. Before and after, I would feel anxious, and it would first hit me right in the pit of my stomach. I would feel nauseous and then as if my throat were closing in on me. My breathing would become uneven, labored. I would feel depleted, defeated, and not good enough. Each time, my engine would be operating on all cylinders in order to accomplish the task at hand. I would get into "beast mode" with a finely tuned tunnel vision to get the job done as close to perfect as possible. The end result: I would feel good for a few moments when someone would compliment my work or share their delight and awe. I would be rewarded for my hard work by getting promotions, rewards, or winning someone's favor or friendship, but the sense of satisfaction would be short-lived, and I would quickly move on to the next task to try and feed the unquenchable thirst for approval.

Reconstructing Ourselves

After I had filled up about half of my journal with what I felt was a real delamination of my layered makeup and driving behaviors, I took a pause for a few days. I felt content with the results of this deconstruction. I was able to correlate many events and motivators in my life to the beliefs that I unearthed and the truths I was finally willing to admit to myself. Then, about a week after I had closed the journal, I returned to the table, flipped it over to the back cover, rotated it, and opened it up to the last page, turning it into the first page. I grabbed my pen and jotted down a new set of prompts:

→ How can I more productively define success?
I can stop comparing myself to others.
I can give people an opportunity when in a team setting to bring their own skills and talents to the table. I can do my best in each moment. I can recognize that I don't have to be the best just do my best.

→ Why am I motivated to change this belief?

I want to feel worthy, feel authentic, feel like a human and have the permission to feel into the spectrum of all human emotions. I don't want to compare myself to anyone any more. I am me. No one else is.

→ When I feel physically activated in response to my belief, how will I choose to respond instead?

When I feel sick to my stomach or shortness of breath due to anxiety, then I will pause and drop into my breathing exercises. I will repeat this mantra to myself: I have enough. I do enough. I am enough.

→ How will I measure my progress?

I will write down what is acceptable and good enough that is associated with each project or event I am involved in. My mark of "success" will identify what is acceptable and achievable. I will take the time to measure my 'success' and to celebrate even the achievements that are good enough.

→ What will motivate me to continue on this path?

The small and large celebrations of every task accomplished even if its not perfect. I will celebrate doing my best in each moment regardless of the outcome. I will allow myself pauses and work on saying no to things.

For three straight weeks, day after day, I responded to these prompts. I liken the process to wearing down a new path in a dense field that eventually led me to a clearing. I knew that I was giving away my power when I compared myself to others, and that each person brings their own set of skills and talents to the table. I was able to articulate that I only had to *do my best* in each moment, which is completely different from trying to *be the best*. I homed in on the moments where the walls would begin to close in on me, having identified my triggers in the previous exercise, and I outlined clear and tangible ways that I would respond instead — with new default modes. In my journal, I resolved that whenever I would sense the onset of that knot in my stomach and felt an accompanying shortness of breath, I would pause and drop into my breathing exercises. I would not only compliment others more often, but every time I walked into a bathroom, I would wash my hands, look in the mirror, and tell myself this mantra, even if I didn't believe it to be true in that moment: *I have enough. I do enough. I am enough.* For each project or event — social or professional — I would clearly and formally (by writing it down!) identify what was "good enough" and acceptable. This set my mark of success at an achievable level, one where I could feel at ease with the tasks before me. I would prolong the celebration of my achievements, and I would not flagellate myself if the output was not the best. I promised myself that I would always do *my* best in every moment.

I challenged my cognitive processes each day and began to reformulate my thoughts, my responses, and therefore, my world. After the three weeks were up, I continued journaling and using my mantra. Old habits die hard. The new path I had begun to forge had to be well-worn in order to become standard practice. *I have enough. I do enough. I am enough.* It's not just a mantra; it's truly a lifestyle.

The moral of all this is both bitter and sweet. As soon as I accepted my ancestral lineage as enough, I was able to understand that my ancestors were fundamental building blocks who had completed their part of our collective journey. This journey will also not be completed by me. I can continue, enhance, and expand it, and then my descendants will do their part. As soon as I accepted myself as enough, I accepted my own limitations and the limitations of life itself, which also meant that I could finally learn to access life's real opportunities. Freedom comes through awareness, and awareness comes through questioning the narratives in our head. After breaking down my walls of false narratives, I consciously chose to reconstruct myself in more realistic ways. This might have felt smaller but it was actually more open. Accepting good enough is actually better. What I learned with each word I wrote is that when we choose to accept ourselves as good enough, we are choosing a better way of being who we already are.

I often find myself wondering how much healing my mother and grandmother, and all the women who came before them, might have done if they'd had the time, the space, the tools, and the encouragement to do so. I am firm in the belief, as I stand at the front lines of our ancestry and predecessors, that bringing healing to the wounds that have been reproducing themselves for generations is not a burden. It is a gift and an honor, an opportunity to contribute to those who may never know my name.

I did not start this process of deconstruction and reconstruction out of some random act of courage. The impetus was a life-altering event. Before I had the wherewithal to sit down and start this spiritual and mental exfoliation, I had to experience something jarring and frightening: complete darkness.

CHAPTER THREE

Not Broken

*All beautiful things carry distinctions of imperfection.
Your wounds and imperfections are your beauty. Like the broken
pottery mended with gold, we are all Kintsugi. It's [a Japanese]
philosophy and art state that all breakages are honest parts of the
past which should not be hidden. Your wounds and healing
are part of your history, a part of who you are. Every beautiful
thing is damaged. You are that beauty; we all are.*

— Bryant McGill

Darkness. In the early hours on a typical midweek spring morning in 2005, I opened my eyes, grasping for my cell phone in order to turn off the obnoxiously loud alarm. I was lying in the guest bedroom, where I had been sleeping each night for months, separated from my (now ex) husband but still living under the same roof in an on-again, off-again pattern. My son, Liam, barely three years old, was lying in the next room, still sound asleep. I reached for the phone in the dark but couldn't find it. I couldn't understand why it would still be dark at 6 a.m. I blinked several times, tightly squeezing my eyes shut and then opening them widely. Open. Close. Open. Close. Open. Still nothing.

Was I dreaming? Sitting up at the edge of the air mattress, I pinched my thigh as hard as I could to confirm that I was indeed awake. I felt every bit of the pain in that spot, but it also reverberated to the rest of my body. My heart started to race. I wasn't even sure I could stand up without fainting from feeling so light-headed. I slowly walked in the direction of where I perceived the door to be, arms outstretched in front of me, feeling for the wall, still holding on to my phone. I couldn't see a thing.

My husband was already gone that morning; he had an early tee time for a round of golf. I crouched down to the floor with my back along the wall of the hallway, right outside of the bathroom door. I didn't want to wake Liam. I needed help. I felt my way around the raised keypad of my Nokia 3310. Having used it thousands of times, I had enough familiarity to navigate the ten digits I needed to press. "Please let this be the right number," I whispered to the heavens and hit the call button. I slowly raised the phone to my right ear. I heard a ringing on the other end and then a familiar voice answered.

"Hello?" It was my friend Gilda. Her daughters were in the same preschool as Liam; her daughter Sophia was in his class.

"Oh my God! Thank God, it's you!" I felt warm teardrops gather in the corners of my eyes.

"What's up? Are you okay? Is everything okay?"

"No, it's not. I need you to come by, please, after you drop the girls off at school. I can't see."

"What do you mean you can't see?"

"I mean…I…um…." I paused, unable to get the words out.

I had a lump in my throat. Finally, I muttered, "I'm blind." Tears streamed down my cheeks as I repeated, "I think I'm blind."

"What? What do you mean? You can't see *anything*?"

"No. Not a thing. I have to go to the hospital. You have to come get me. I don't know what to do. I can't call 911 — it will scare Liam. I can't even get dressed." The sound of urgency in my voice was apparent.

Gilda, always the right person to call in an emergency, reassuringly said, "If you can't see, we need to go to an ophthalmologist. I know a good one. Try to stay calm. I'll be there as soon as possible. Don't worry."

"I'll try," I said as I gasped for breath. It was an outright lie. I crawled on all fours toward Liam's room, eventually making my way to his bed and reaching up to pull myself to my knees. I could hear him breathing. I moved toward the sound and eventually felt the warm outbreath from his nostrils. I started to kiss his face gently, as I did every morning to wake him — his sweet cheeks, his forehead, the creases in his neck, his button nose. "Good morning, my love," I managed to get out as tears streamed down my face and certainly hit his face as well. I felt the weight of his tiny arm wrap around my neck, his hand on the back of my head, pulling me in for a snuggle. I was usually in a rush to get him to school and head to work, but that morning I just laid there and took in the moment as the realization seeped in that I might never see my son's beautiful face again.

"Eema," my son whispered in my ear, his familiar voice calling me "Mom" in Hebrew. "Do you have a boo-boo?" he asked.

"Yes," I replied. "Eema has a boo-boo and needs to go see a doctor today. But we will have an adventure this morning! Sophia's mommy is going to take us to school, and you are going to be a big boy and help Eema by picking out your clothes and helping to get dressed this morning. Can you do that?"

"Yes! I can be a big boy!" Liam said with excitement. "You look! I can be a big boy!" He sat up and got out of bed. I could hear his tiny footsteps going toward the bathroom, then a faint flushing of the toilet and the water running in the sink. Minutes later, as I sat on the floor near the bed, I heard him walk back into the room and then felt his hand pulling mine. "Come!" he said.

Liam walked me to the dresser. He managed to open the drawer, and I instructed him to pull out his clothes, *anything* he wanted to wear to school that day. I got his pajama top off, and feeling for the shirt tag, I helped him put on a T-shirt. In the top right drawer, I grabbed a pair of underwear and held them out; he steadied himself by grabbing my shoulders and put one leg in at a time. I managed somehow to get him dressed, albeit slowly. In fact, not only did the deeply ingrained, familiar motions of being Liam's mom help me that morning, it was the only thing that eventually saved me from the mess that was then my life.

We slowly scooted down the stairs, poured a "big boy" bowl of cereal, and no sooner had Liam announced, "I'm done!" than we heard a knock at the front door. Once I managed to get the front door open, I was greeted by a sweet voice and floral perfume.

"Hey, there! Can you see me?" Gilda asked, holding on to my shoulders, as we stood face to face.

"Not at all."

"Ugh," she groaned, stepping into action. There was no time to waste. "Okay, what do you need me to grab? Where is your bag? Liam's backpack?" She walked past me into the living room. "Hi, Liam! You ready to go to school? Come show me where your shoes are, let's go upstairs and get them together." I heard footsteps on the stairs getting fainter.

"My mommy has a boo-boo," Liam said to Gilda.

"Yes, I know. But don't worry! We are going to make sure it's all taken care of and that she will feel all better soon," Gilda reassured him.

"Gilda!" I yelled up the stairs. "Grab me some sweats, socks, and a pair of sneakers from my closet, please."

"Okay!"

Gilda saved me that day. She showed up for me in every way. She called my workplace to let them know that I was having a medical emergency and wouldn't be able to come in, she got me dressed, and she got Liam to preschool. I waited in the car as she walked Liam into school; she also let the school office know that she might be picking him up later. She drove me to an ophthalmologist, carefully walked me inside, and stayed to help me fill out all my paperwork as a new patient. Once I heard my name called, Gilda and I linked arms and shuffled into the examination room, where Gilda sat me down on the leather chair. As I leaned my head back, the nurse dilated my eyes with several drops. "Dr. Weiner will be right with you," she said, and then left.

"I'm freaking out," I confided to Gilda, breaking the silence.

"I know," she acknowledged, letting her emotions show. "I would be, too. Just breathe. Let's breathe together." She put her hand in mine, and we rhythmically inhaled deeply and exhaled fully. Reflecting back, I am pretty certain that in that moment my meditation muscle memory started to come back to me. After graduate school, life became riddled with obligations, and I fell away from practice. First, I would miss a day here and there, then weeks at a time, and eventually, I became what might be called a "crisis meditator" — a person who returns to the practice only when the going gets tough. Eventually, I stopped meditating altogether; it was not something that I ever thought I would resurrect.

That first long, slow, deep in-breath was like turning the key in the ignition of a vehicle that had sat idle for several years. In that moment, the engine to the old car didn't exactly turn over, but something reconnected. Contact had been made.

The door opened. "Hi, Shelly. I'm Dr. Weiner. Let's see what's going on here today." Dr. Weiner sounded like an older man. He had a New York accent, and I imagined he looked like a Jewish grandpa — white hair, kind eyes, prominent nose, bushy eyebrows. I could smell him and sense that he was close to my face. He must have been looking directly in my eyes with his light and magnification scope. "Hmmm," he hummed. "This is interesting...very interesting." The wheels of his chair squeaked across the floor as he picked up a receiver. "Dr. Feldman, can you come into room four when you have a moment? I have something *very interesting* to show you.... Okay, thanks."

In my head, my thoughts were like a five-alarm fire. I felt doomed as I sunk down into the chair and further into myself. The door squeaked open.

"Hello, there," said a much-too-enthusiastic voice. "I'm Dr. Feldman. What are we looking at here, Dr. Weiner?"

"Well, pull up a chair and see for yourself," said Dr. Weiner. Chair wheels slid toward me. I could smell Dr. Feldman as he drew close to my face.

"Ah, I see," said Dr. Feldman. "Looks like uveitis to me and an incredibly active case at that. Lots of inflammation. I can barely see in there. I imagine she can barely see out."

"She can't," squawked Gilda from the back of the room. "She can't see out."

"Are you experiencing any other symptoms?" one of the doctors said, finally addressing me directly.

"Like what?" I replied.

"Pain or stiffness in your joints, your back, spine, maybe an unusual prolonged fatigue."

"No, not really. Just this."

Dr. Feldman and Dr. Weiner conferred, speaking in medical lingo that was foreign to me. When I heard the words "cannot treat here," I immediately spoke up in a panicked voice. "Excuse me, what do you mean? It's not treatable?!"

"Well," said Dr. Weiner, "we cannot treat you here. It's too severe. The bad news is that you have a chronic autoimmune condition called uveitis. Yours has been active clearly for quite some time. Because it has gone untreated or undetected, it may have done some irreparable harm. The good news is that the number one eye hospital in the country is just a short drive from here. A specialist there who deals with this disease — Dr. Janet Davis — is the absolute best person, probably in the world. I will send her an email and refer you, and I'll let her know it's urgent. You must go see her as soon as possible."

"What is uveitis, doctor?" asked Gilda, as I sat like a possum, frozen from fear.

"It's actually not as uncommon as you think," Dr. Weiner replied. "Lots of people have uveitis, although it's usually associated with other autoimmune diseases, like AIDS, multiple sclerosis, or ankylosing spondylitis. This is why I asked her if she was experiencing other symptoms. Basically, your brain is telling your eyes there is an infection, in your case in the vitreous, which is the gel-like fluid that fills your eye. This is where floaters that you can blink away usually are. When there is an infection, just like everywhere in the body, white blood cells rush in to save the day. But in this case, in the eyes, your white blood cells have become so engorged that they rush in, but they are too big to circulate out. I suspect that you have some leakage happening in the back of the eye, too. The capillaries are probably leaking into the eye cavity. But Dr. Davis can confirm that for you. You'll need to have special imaging done. Uveitis — it's actually one of the leading causes of blindness in people under the age of forty."

If Dr. Weiner said anything after that sentence, I have no recollection of it. The world was physically dark already, but in that moment, things went emotionally dark. I felt as if a black hole had opened up beneath my feet and just pulled me in. On the ride back home, I called my mother to share the news. I then called my soon-to-be ex-husband to ask him to pick up Liam on the way home. Gilda insisted on grabbing me something to eat before dropping me off, but I wasn't hungry at all. Once I was home, I simply crawled into bed, closed my eyes, and noticed the rare sound of silence. The absence of light existed everywhere: in my ears, in my eyes, in my heart. I wished myself to sleep, so that I could wake up and realize that it was all just a dream. But when I woke up hours later, I realized that it was not a dream.

Thanks to Dr. Weiner's concern and advocacy, I got an appointment with Dr. Davis the next day. After dropping Liam at preschool, my mother drove me to Bascom Palmer Eye Institute. We spent most of the day waiting as I was moved from waiting area to waiting area, and from exam room to exam room, as people took images and then poked and prodded me. When I finally saw Dr. Davis, she confirmed my diagnosis — uveitis, specifically a type called pars planitis. She wanted me to see a rheumatologist to make sure that I didn't have an early onset of some other type of autoimmune disease, one that would slowly take the use of my body away, too.

Then Dr. Davis said she wanted to inject my eyeballs directly with the steroid prednisone. I would be awake for this, and the only fortunate part of not being able to see was that I wouldn't know when the needle was coming toward my eye. Prednisone would help relieve the symptoms but not cure the root cause of the disease. It would help me see again, she said, by shrinking the engorged white blood cells so that they could circulate out of the eye again. Afterward, I would need to be on systemic medication forever (orally or intravenously), and I would need to have a laser treatment to help with the leakage in the capillaries behind my eye. I could barely process anything that she told me. In less than forty-eight hours, my entire life had changed. And it could possibly get even worse — if I got diagnosed with another rheumatic illness. I felt like I was in the darkest pit in the world and someone was about to close the top, sealing my fate.

I was twenty-seven years old. This was not how I had planned things. *This cannot be it*, I thought. *It just can't*. I wanted to scream at the top of my lungs, but nothing would come out. I was like a robot, just going through the motions, being led by the arm. After my injections, my eyes swelled and were burning so much I thought they were on fire. Dr. Davis said I would experience gradual improvement in my sight as the steroid was absorbed over time, but in that moment, I was still blind.

When I got home that evening, Liam was already bathed and in his pajamas. He could see that my eyes were swollen shut. I could hear in his voice the sense of concern and empathy. I asked him to lead me upstairs, and my mother followed — she helped me change into my pajamas and wash my face, and then I crawled into bed with Liam, allowing him to rest his head on my chest.

"Eema, tell me a story," he said.

"Okay, Liam, sure. Once upon a time there was a little girl who lost her way but found herself...." I rambled on for several minutes until I could hear his heavy breathing and knew he was sound asleep. I left his head where it lay, closed my eyes, and said a prayer for the first time in years to whoever might be listening.

The next morning, I attempted to open my eyes ever so slowly, but the lashes were stuck together. I gently rubbed my eyes to separate the lids, and when I opened my eyes, I could see color and light. I could see the blurry outline of my son's face. When I got close enough, I could make out the details of his face as he slumbered. Ever so grateful, I remembered that experience in Dr. Weiner's office when Gilda helped me calm down, and I tried to turn the key again in that dusty car's old ignition. I remembered to breathe.

Feel It 'til You Heal It

I once saw a greeting card in a local shop, written and illustrated by artist Emily McDowell from the brand Em & Friends. It read:

> "Finding yourself" is not how it really works. You aren't a ten-dollar bill in last winter's coat pocket. You are not lost. Your true self is right there, buried under cultural conditioning, other people's opinions, and inaccurate conclusions you drew as a kid that became your beliefs about who you are. "Finding yourself" is actually returning to yourself. An unlearning, an excavation, a remembering who you were before the world got its hands on you.

This statement resonated so deeply with me that I bought the entire allotment of cards displayed on the rack. I kept the cards in my desk drawer for a few months, peaking at them every so often. When I moved into my own place, I framed one for myself, and I eventually sent the rest to people I thought needed to hear this message so that they, too, could be reminded that sometimes when we are buried, we may feel like we are dead, but we're not. We are seeds.

Right after I was diagnosed with my chronic eye disease, there was no relief, only fear of "what else do I have?" Several doctors took me down the rabbit hole of trying to figure out if I was afflicted with another disease, and most confirmed my worst fear — that my eye disease was a byproduct of something else. My rheumatologist was like Sherlock Holmes, looking for clues that were present and some that were not ever there. In the end, he settled on the diagnosis of acute ankylosing spondylitis; I tested positive for a genetic marker that is present in many people who have it (but not all), and I had an incident with tendonitis in my ankle a few months before. He gave me a few pamphlets to read and proposed a course of action: I would take a fairly new medicine being used to treat patients with various autoimmune conditions that required a once-per-month, in-office intravenous infusion. I didn't question the diagnosis or the course of treatment. His words washed over me; my brain was in as much of a fog as my eyes.

When I got home that evening, I searched "ankylosing spondylitis" on the internet, where I learned that, over time, this inflammatory disease can cause the small bones in your spine to fuse. As the vertebrae fuse, the spine becomes less flexible, and if the ribs are affected, it can make breathing difficult. Seeing photos of people with an advanced progression of the disease made me feel broken. Ready to give up. I couldn't imagine being blind, unable to walk, and possibly unable to breathe. My current living arrangement was toxic, and I knew I could not count on or expect my soon-to-be ex-husband to take care of me. If I didn't have my son, I'm not sure that I would be here today telling you my story.

Quite robotically, I decided to follow the protocols prescribed by my doctors, which was the only way I knew how to get better. I couldn't think clearly, and I had no faith in my ability to direct my own health or treatment. My only real hope was to prolong whatever "good years" I had left to make an impact on my son. I had no expectation of making an impact in this world beyond that. I crawled back into Liam's bed that night, and after he fell asleep on my chest, I remembered being a freshman in that undergraduate philosophy class and studying Viktor Frankl. According to Frankl, there was one thing I could control: my mental state. I also remembered that, unlike my mother and her mother before her, I had the agency to leave the environment I was in.

The very next day, I started to look for a new place to live. I wanted to change my physical surroundings so that I could focus on my mental health. I resolved to complete my move two weeks before receiving my first infusion. I also made the commitment to myself to begin journaling again each day, a habit I had stopped years earlier. That day, my friend Helen drove me to the bookstore to pick up some books about how to heal autoimmune conditions. I only walked out with one thing: a bright red, lined journal.

This was the first sentence I wrote in the journal when I sat down that day: "I AM NOT BROKEN." I looked up at the mirror across from the dining room, my eyesight better each day as the inflammation gradually dissipated. I stared myself down. "I am not broken," I said out loud to myself. Then I wrote: "But I feel broken and I won't be broken forever." This was the first time I admitted I was struggling. Long before that dark morning, I had spent years lying to myself, covering up for the misery I was feeling, and pretending like I was fine and that my marriage was fine. Admitting this was important because it was the first time I acknowledged that what I was experiencing emotionally was real but that it did not define me and it did not have to be permanent. I gave myself permission that day to "feel it 'til I heal it."

Normally, whenever I experienced any negative emotions, I would try to resist or ignore them. I would think to myself, *I shouldn't be feeling angry*, or *I don't want to feel hurt*. I would compartmentalize my emotions and put them away, telling myself I'd deal with them at another, more convenient time. This harmful resistance came naturally to me — I did it to protect myself — but in the end it only masked the truth, created more suffering, and resulted in a physical illness. Now my boxed emotions were bursting open, and I had to deal with the contents at, ironically, the most inconvenient time of all.

The Two Types of Happiness

Today, I realize that I wasn't happy because I was focused on the wrong kind of happiness. There are actually two kinds of happiness: One is conditional. It comes from the positive experiences we have. It's fleeting, and it leaves as soon as something bad happens. The other is sustainable and unconditional. It doesn't depend on a singular event. It remains steadfast during pleasant and undesirable experiences. This is the type of happiness that has been described as the canvas upon which all other emotions are painted.

The path to conditional happiness is pretty self-explanatory and one most people are familiar with. It depends on meeting certain conditions — developing a healthy morning routine, achieving certain types of success, reaching particular goals, cultivating positive thinking. But I have always found that positive thinking as a consistent habit is downright impossible. It's exhaustingly hard and taxing because controlling our thoughts is hard. Our brains constantly produce thoughts, which come and go and shift. Further, when we believe and latch on to our thoughts, we live them out in our experience. When our thoughts seem real, we bring them to life. In other words: Our feelings tend to reflect our inner world, perceptions, or consciousness, not what our circumstances are in the outer world.

For instance, have you ever walked into a dimly lit room and mistaken a coat on a hanger for an intruder? For a moment, your heart beats out of your chest as your fight-flight-freeze reaction kicks in. Then, as your eyes adjust or you flick on the light, you see it is a coat and laugh, realizing you were safe the whole time. Yet the only thing that changed was your perception, your thoughts.

This profound notion applies to any negative thought. Most of the time, we try to simply banish negative thoughts; that's what conventional wisdom tells us to do. Be happy; practice positive thinking. But standing in the dark telling ourselves not to be afraid almost never works. Because here is the thing: It isn't our job to change our thoughts. The mind rapidly produces new thoughts in reaction to whatever is happening (or to whatever we perceive is happening), so we should let thoughts naturally pass in and out of our consciousness. If we obstruct thoughts, we actually keep them from leaving; we hold on to them. Instead, we can use our consciousness like a light switch. We can shift away from focusing on *what* we think (there's an intruder), and observe the fact *that* we think (I feel afraid), and this act of observation helps us see when fear is only fear. We can't stop our thoughts, but this process helps us recognize that we aren't our thoughts and we aren't our beliefs or perceptions. We don't need to reprogram ourselves or try to think only positive thoughts.

Of course, with little nuisances and minor daily challenges, it's easy to recognize the transient nature of negative thoughts and let them go. This is harder in the most important and stressful areas of our lives, but it doesn't make the principle any less true. Childhood trauma, illness, destructive patterns of behavior, bad marriages, dysfunctional families — these areas cause the *most* suffering because we latch on to our painful thoughts about these experiences. We don't let these feelings go, and so they become real and hellish, as if we were trapped in class-5 whitewater rapids that we are madly trying to escape. For years, I was caught in this maelstrom; my thoughts became heavy stones I thought would sink me. I would most often stow them away when they became too intense and not deal with them, but when I did finally decide to deal with them, they seemed real and scary and caused me an immense amount of suffering. Eventually, though, I learned to observe these thoughts and not treat them as real, and they always passed; I would be carried to a calmer part of the river where I could reach the banks. But in the moments when I was stuck in the whirlpool, I couldn't imagine that I would ever get to a riverbank again. I was struggling to just tread water and survive.

This is the same thing that happens in the analogy of the intruder: If we turn on the light or see the situation differently, fear often disappears on its own. This transformation is possible with any pain that we experience over and over again. I found myself latching on to many painful thoughts: *I am broken, I am going to be blind soon, I am preconditioned to think this way because of my family history and the way I was raised, My marriage is a sham and*

I am a failure, and so on. Yet I came to recognize that if I changed my perception of these problems, or if I saw even the worst experiences in a different light, I experienced them differently. I felt set free. I found I could use recognition of my own agency to dislodge myself from being stuck, and in some instances, I could move to action.

For me, this started in the moment when I said to myself: "I am not broken." Now, when I feel myself becoming stuck in fear, I remember how the mind works: Thoughts arise in reaction to perceptions, and I experience them as real. But if I become conscious and aware of my thoughts and perceptions (sometimes I write them down so I can be fully conscious of them), and allow thoughts to float in and out on their own, I become less scared. This way, I avoid becoming paralyzed by my thoughts and can move to action.

In other words, I finally understood that I was not broken; I only felt broken, and that feeling was temporary and would not last forever. Nor was I a victim of my ancestral lineage; I wasn't forced to repeat someone else's mistakes. I had agency, and I could change some of my circumstances. For instance, I did not have to continue living in the house that my ex-husband and I were fighting over, and so I did not. In time, the more I allowed myself to see the transient, thought-created nature of my experiences, the more I was able to pave the way for a simple, unconditional happiness to awaken, one that is not in opposition to negative experiences. This state of being became the stillness underneath any emotion on the choppy surface of agitated waters.

CHAPTER FOUR

Familiarization

Knowing yourself is the beginning of all wisdom.

— ARISTOTLE

It's remarkable what can happen when just one ball is set in motion. Within a month of my diagnosis, I finalized the terms of my divorce and found a townhouse to rent. In our new rental, Liam and I settled in nicely with the help of dear friends who helped to unpack boxes, brought meals, and gave us their extra towels, linens, and kitchenware. For the first week, the busyness and constant comings-and-goings of people helped to fill up the hole in my heart. My eyesight had been restored due to the prednisone treatments, but I was not out of the woods, since white blood cells were continuing to reaccumulate in my eyes with each passing day, and the capillaries continued to leak. I also resigned myself to the diagnosis of ankylosing spondylitis. I was scheduled to begin my intravenous treatments within two weeks of our move-in date.

It's hard for me to aptly explain that time period. During those two weeks, I felt like I was recalibrating. As if, as I unpacked my physical possessions, I was simultaneously unpacking my mental baggage. I felt like a snow globe that had been violently shaken for years, never allowed to settle, and yet finally, I was starting to see the glitter float gently to the bottom. Everything happened both swiftly and in slow motion. I still had a preschooler to tend to and a full-time job, but it was miraculous how much more time and space I had to think, pause, and just be. Almost every morning, before waking up Liam for the day, I would rise with the sun and sit at the small table in my new kitchen and open up my bright red journal, and each night, after reading Liam a bedtime story and watching him fall asleep, I would quietly creep to the living room — some nights almost crawling — to my meditation cushion. During these hours, I was formally becoming reacquainted with myself.

One of my favorite words in Tibetan is *göm*, or "meditation," which is derived from a word that actually means "familiarization." In a way, I was refamiliarizing myself with the occupant of my physical body. I think that most people think that meditation is an excavation, a sort of "clearing out," but what I've found is that it's not really about removing anything. It's about taking inventory, "familiarizing" ourselves with even the darkest corners of our mind, and learning to coexist with what we find. It's about learning to relegate some of the key boxes to long-term storage, others to the closet in the guest room, and some to the attic or basement where they will collect dust. We can't "Marie Kondo" these boxes — or dump the ones that don't bring us joy or take them to Goodwill. They aren't of use to anyone else, and they remain the fragments and cracks and stories and memories that make us who we are. Even if we attempt to burn them in a fire, we can't because they are imprinted on our cells and encoded in our DNA. If we aren't careful, we will pass even the most terrifying imprints on to our descendants. It is our job to familiarize ourselves with what's there, understand where it came from, and organize it in a manner that creates a clearing for shifts that will heal us.

Initially, I found leaning into a daily meditation practice again to be incredibly challenging. Some days, I would become even more triggered by my time on the cushion than in my moments off of it. I hadn't meditated regularly for close to a decade, ever since I was a graduate student and a young woman beginning her career. Before I could refamiliarize myself with Shelly, I had to refamiliarize myself with the practice of meditation itself. The specific core practice I studied is called *metta bhavana*, which comes from the Pali language. First used in India in the third century, Pali is widely used in Buddhist scriptures and still studied for that reason. *Metta* means "love," in a nonromantic sense, or kindness, and *bhavana* means cultivation or development. This form of "loving-kindness" meditation practice helps the practitioner cultivate compassion, and on a personal level, it has helped me define what the verb form of the words *love, kindness,* and *compassion* mean; it's helped me to love myself, too.

What does love have to do with meditation, which is usually focused on the mind? First, in most Eastern languages, the words for "heart" and "mind" are the same, and meditation practices usually see no distinction. Meditation is a tool used to train mind and heart, since we can never dissociate the heart from the mind. "The heart" certainly takes over when we feel love, leading us to sometimes do very questionable things. The core of meditation practice in its truest sense is a deep mindfulness — a heartfelt knowing. As the nineteenth-century Sikh leader Ranjit Singh once said, "Sometimes the heart knows things the mind could never explain."

The cushion I sat on each evening had been stored in the garage of my former house, behind a defunct toaster oven, a box of books, and old tax returns. The first time I sat on it in my new home — after first pounding the dust out of it in the front yard, of course — I was reminded of how I first came to learn about meditation and about loving-kindness practice.

In 1998, I took an internship with the "Transition Team" in Geneva, Switzerland, at the World Health Organization. Dr. Gro Harlem Brundtland, the former prime minister of Norway, had just become the first female director-general of the organization. I had just finished my first year as a graduate student at the School of International and Public Affairs at Columbia University in New York City, and I wanted to spend the summer in a meaningful way that would make me more attractive to employers upon graduation the following year. I arrived at the communal, dorm-style housing facility as a skinny, almost-twenty-year-old Orthodox Jewish girl who prayed three times a day — morning, afternoon, and evening — in compliance with the standards of the *halachahs*, or rabbinic laws. For modesty reasons, I wore only long skirts below the knee and shirts that covered my collar bones and elbows. I ate only foods that were deemed kosher by an Orthodox rabbi. I followed the "39 laws" of the Sabbath starting every Friday night at sundown; for a period of twenty-four hours, I wasn't allowed to turn on the lights, cook, shower, ride in a car, write or draw, or "create" or "destroy" anything.

I wish I could say that each Sabbath spent in observance was meaningful for me or somehow enhanced my week, the day itself, or my life in general. If anything, being an Orthodox Jewish girl allowed me to be part of a community and helped provide some order to the universe. I didn't have to think so hard about everything because most things were already defined for me: what I wore, what I ate, which shoe I put on first in the morning, who I could marry, and even what to say when I left the bathroom after washing my hands. But to say that I had *kavanah* — which means "intention," or a sincere feeling or direction of the heart — would be a lie. Throughout my life I questioned the existence of a personal God, the way I was taught to believe in Him. But to live in the world I grew up in and believe in Him was a far easier existence than to rebel against Him. For the girl who felt she never belonged to anything to actually have some place, some set of beliefs, and some people to belong to meant everything.

Each morning in Switzerland, I woke up at the crack of dawn in my tiny little room, with slate floors and a wooden desk and bed, window cracked open to smell the fresh, crisp mountain air. I washed my face in the room's small sink, threw on a cotton skirt over my pajama pants, grabbed my *sidur* (prayer book), and headed to the front porch of the central building. The view from that porch was exquisite. It was literally everything I imagined Switzerland should be. On a clear day I could see the surrounding mountain range, Lake Geneva below, and green upon green for miles and miles. If I was to have a reckoning with God, it should have been on that mountaintop, truly one of His finest creations. Then I opened to the ticked and well-worn page of my morning prayers and began to recite them in a rote manner, my mind wandering to my to-do list, to breakfast, to the day ahead.

On the third morning, I noticed that I was not alone. Sitting on the corner of the wooden deck was a couple — a man and a woman of Asian descent — with their legs dangling over the side, bare feet crossed at the ankles and resting in the grass below. I had not seen them before in any of the common areas where many of us would gather in the early evenings. The whole scene was peculiar to me, as I slowly tip-toed a bit closer, at an angle where I could clearly see them but they couldn't see me. From this vantage point, I realized that their eyes were closed. They were just sitting there… doing nothing? Strange. I opened up my prayer book to the same page I did each morning and focused on the same task. About twenty minutes in, the couple opened their eyes, slowly stood up, and walked past me toward the front door of the main building. I caught the eyes of the woman, and she grinned at me and nodded as I grinned back. The quality of her aura was intense. I know that sounds like complete bullshit, but something in the intensity of her presence made me pause in the middle of reciting my morning prayers. My immediate thought was, *How can I get some of that?* I felt equal parts curious and jealous.

I later learned they were a newly married couple, Suki and Hiroto, who had just arrived in Geneva via Tokyo to begin their jobs with UNICEF and the World Bank, respectively. This was a place for them to land for a few weeks as they searched for a long-term, more centrally located apartment. Each morning they practiced Zen meditation, "focusing on their posture, breath awareness, and the quality of their mind." I wrote that specific phrase in my notebook when sitting one evening with Suki, having a cup of tea. I was as fascinated by her as she was by me, since she had never met someone Jewish, let alone someone from Israel who was obser-vant of the religious laws. Those encounters with Suki and Hiroto planted a seed for me. I learned that in order to meditate, I didn't need to be a monk. I learned that I didn't need to be sitting on a mountaintop (though we were in fact on a mountaintop). I didn't need to be in an ashram or temple. I didn't need to wear an orange or red robe or chant anything. I also learned from Suki that she was an atheist, so I didn't even need to believe in God to be able to meditate. What I ruminated on for months after our encounter — what bothered me to no end — was the fact that the purpose of my thrice-daily contemplative practice was supposed to be meditative in nature, a meditation on a higher being but also a cleansing of my own soul. Instead, I found that after each obligation was fulfilled, I felt emptier and less connected to myself and to the world. However, I had an image to uphold, I had peers in the community to which I *belonged*, and I could not let anyone down. I aimed to please. I aimed to please everyone but myself, that is.

Returning to Columbia University for the fall semester, while selecting classes, I found myself leafing through the pages of the course directory under the Religion department. I had already selected the fifteen credits I needed to fulfill my masters of public policy degree, but a full-tuition payment allowed me to take up to twenty-one credits. I decided to audit a class to learn more about Buddhism and meditation. Mostly because of my available schedule, I landed on a class about Indo-Tibetan Buddhism taught by Professor Robert Thurman. I had never heard of Robert Thurman, and thus I did not connect the dots to realize he is Uma Thurman's father. I also did not realize he is part of the thriving Free Tibet movement championed by influential people like actor Richard Gere, composer Philip Glass, and musicians Patti Smith, Iggy Pop, and Natalie Merchant. The only thing that informed my decision was that I had been entrusted with a seed by Suki and Hiroto and I knew I needed to nurture it.

Since I was auditing the class for no credit, I did not have to do the assignments or take tests. I was allowed to attend the class, and I had access to the instructor and the learning materials. For me, the class was a journey of both discovery and rediscovery. That is, I felt a familiarity that I couldn't comprehend and still can't fully explain. I experienced a "knowing," or an affirmation of sorts, that just told me I was in the right place. Attending that class was not easy for me. I was terribly worried about how my Orthodox Jewish peers and the community-at-large would judge me for investing my time and efforts to learn about what they considered to be an idolatrous faith. This was time I could have been spending studying the Torah. It should have felt sacrilegious to merely be sitting in that class, but instead I felt a sense of expansion.

During one lecture, Dr. Thurman described spearheading the efforts to build Tibet House in New York City, a physical center founded at the request of the Dalai Lama. Its mission is to preserve, present, and protect Tibet's ancient traditions and culture, which are still being threatened by the Chinese invasion of Tibet. Dr. Thurman left a few flyers and schedules up at the front of the classroom and mentioned that the center offered free lectures, workshops, and meditation classes. This announcement caught my attention — specifically the words *meditation classes* — and so I grabbed a flyer and stuffed it in my trench coat on the way out. When I arrived home later that evening, I pulled the flyer out and took a closer look — the center was in the historic Chelsea district, over a hundred city blocks from the Columbia University campus. At that location, there was a slim chance of someone recognizing me. I turned the flyer over to review the schedule of offerings for the month and resolved to head down the following week to one of the classes.

The day I went, I stepped out of the subway somewhere in

the Chelsea district, a place I hadn't frequented often since arriving in New York City. On West 15th Street, I stood before the entrance and stared at the red brick building and green rust-covered doors. I took a deep breath and walked in behind another woman, who upon entering ran the palm of her hand over a row of prayer wheels, which made a beautiful sound. I walked upstairs to a room with a wooden riser, which was surrounded by pillows on the floor and rows of chairs in the back. I opted to sit in the back, where I continued to sit week after week, returning each time to listen to the same teacher — a woman named Sharon Salzberg. From Sharon's talks, I learned the word *metta*, and through her guidance, I learned to practice loving-kindness meditation. Each week, she led us through a series of visualizations where we sent well-wishes and benevolent and loving energy to ourselves and toward others — strangers, loved ones, and even people we have difficulty with. The first time I practiced loving-kindness, I distinctly remember that when we began to offer happiness, joy, peace, and freedom from suffering to ourselves, I began to cry. It was as if a shield around my heart just cracked open, a shield that I didn't even know existed. For two decades I had prayed and prayed, waiting for my heart to be struck, waiting for the *kavanah* to take root. Here, in one sitting, I found myself emotionally moved to tears.

Each week, I shuffled in and shuffled out, rarely speaking to anyone. Then one day, I walked out at the same time as Sharon. "Hello," she said warmly.

"Hi, Sharon. Thanks for your teachings. I'm Shelly....I sit in the back."

She smiled and responded, "Yeah, I know."

As we neared the entrance door, knowing we would then go

our separate ways, I suddenly found within me a boost of courage to ask her the question that had been weighing on my mind since the first week she introduced herself. "Excuse me, but can I ask you a question?"

"Sure." She stopped walking and turned toward me, looking squarely at my face.

"Um, I know this is going to sound strange but" — I paused and took a deep breath — "are you Jewish?" Salzberg sounded to me like a Jewish last name.

Sharon chuckled and replied, "Well, I am culturally Jewish. I was born to a Jewish family, but I practice Buddhism." As she turned toward the door, she said, "I guess you could say I'm a BuJew."

I don't know what Sharon, in that moment, thought about this exchange. When I've asked her about it in recent years, she says she doesn't even recall it. But for me it was a seminal moment. That half-joke did something incredible — it gave me permission to have duality, to not have to choose to be one thing or the other. I could be Jewish, and I could study Buddhism and meditate. I could familiarize myself with my heart, a place that my young soul had not properly explored yet, and I could use the practice of *metta* to find the entry points into this shielded and protected space. For two years, whenever I could sneak away from schoolwork and obligations, I returned to Tibet House, slowly replacing my traditional morning prayers with a sit instead. I slowly drifted away from traditional practices, finding comfort and hope in the silence of my heart, moving further from the need for a congregation and a scripted verse.

As I sat on the cushion each evening, in a quiet household

with my son asleep upstairs and my yellow Labrador asleep at my feet, I tugged at the overgrown thorny vines around my heart, looking desperately to feel soft again, to reacquaint myself with the permission to heal and revisit the virtual space I needed in order to do it. Some evenings I just sat in silence and focused on my dog's methodic breathing, recognizing that I was in the midst of a shift, a transformation. But like a driver sitting at the wheel with the keys in my hand, I didn't always have the strength to lift the key to the ignition and turn over the engine. Some days, I got the car running but remained in park or neutral because I didn't have the strength to shift gears to drive. There was so much for me to process, so many wrong turns and potential hazards on the roads ahead that I didn't know where to begin. Yet, with Liam as my passenger, I knew that I had to begin somewhere — anywhere. We had made it this far, right?

The first few nights when I sat on my cushion, it did not end well. Too much time had passed since I had fully examined the contents of my brain. I ended up in the darkest recess of my mind, feeling like I was free-falling into a dark, bottomless pit without even a single branch to grasp at. I opened my eyes frequently and stared at the unpacked boxes surrounding me. I thought about the upcoming infusion that was scheduled for the following week and the possible outcomes of my disease, feeling a building anxiety over the fact that I was still expected to somehow accomplish everyday tasks on a daily basis. I was still very much a perpetual people pleaser at this point in my life. This never went away. When I was busy during the day, I could manage because I compartmentalized my emotions. In the silent hours of the night, without the preoccupations of the day's busyness, I felt trapped in a prison and held captive by my thoughts. I was caught between feeling like I still had something to prove to everyone else and the belief that I had nothing left to offer. I had goals, but I did not know how to work toward them or where to even begin; I felt paralyzed.

The Elephant in the Room

Years ago, my business colleagues and I were discussing a strategy for a new large-scale account we were planning on taking over. The start-up was going to be the most complex project we had ever taken on as a team. As we all stared at the blank whiteboard in the conference room, I recall one of my associates saying, "There is so much to do, we don't even know where to begin." One of our executives immediately grabbed the dry-erase marker and walked up to the whiteboard, asking, "How do you eat an elephant?" We all stared blankly at this non sequitur. As he grinned, he answered his own question: "One bite at a time!"

The executive explained that in a college psychology course he learned about a concept called "chunking." Simply put, cognitive psychologists have found that by breaking down a large amount of information into individual related elements, ideas, groups, or tasks, these chunks improve short-term retention of the information, essentially bypassing the limited capacity of working memory. The most common example of chunking is the way phone numbers are written. For example, which phone number seems easier to memorize: 3051324723 or 305-132-4723? People can use chunking for anything, whether to manage everyday life or to tackle big projects and life goals that require many sets of tasks to accomplish.

On the fourth night of my return to meditation practice, I thought of this and asked myself out loud: "How do you eat an elephant?" Then I promptly responded to my own question: "With a pen!" I got up off the cushion, grabbed a pen and paper, and wrote down the following stream of words, in this order:

- Chunking
- Trust
- Shift
- Identity
- Motivation

In that moment I resolved to try and take only one bite at a time and get as much as I could written down so that my brain would feel less overwhelmed trying to remember it all. I captured all of the tasks on my overwhelming to-do list. Overwhelm is one of my main emotional triggers. I found that my stress was significantly alleviated simply by writing tasks down. Then I looked at the list as a whole and began to chunk, or group together, items that were related to one another on the list. I created clusters for areas like physical health, emotional well-being, relationships, career, and finances. Doing this simple exercise helped me envision a clearer path to my purpose; it was as if there was suddenly a clearing in the dense forest. In that moment, I realized that my only intention was to stay healthy in order to be a presence and provider in Liam's life. With that in mind, I evaluated each chunk and wrote down a few bullet points about how each cluster of tasks related to that purpose (see copies of my original lists on the next page).

Shelly To Do List Tomorrow

1. Register Liam for Summer Camp
2. Buy karate uniform for Liam
3. Unpack all kitchen boxes and put them away
4. Develop budget for annual meeting at work
5. Review budget for last quarter/analysis
6. Drop Liam off at karate
7. Pick up Liam from karate
8. Meditate for 20 minutes
9. Dust the downstairs rooms
10. Create meditation plan for month
11. Buy dog food
12. Create carpool schedule for month

Chunk 1 = O = DRIVE | Chunk 3 = □ = SELF-CARE
Chunk 2 = △ = WORK | Chunk 4 = ◇ = CHORES/DAILY TASKS

As I thought of each item on my list as a cluster, and each cluster on my list as a desired outcome supporting my purpose, my anxiety over the minutiae dissipated. If the task at hand did not support my purpose, I didn't allow myself to stress out over it. This simple technique helped me remain inspired, since I was working toward something greater than just a checkmark on a to-do list. Purpose inspires action. This works for everyone. Each time we chunk together many small, similar tasks or break down one large task into smaller and more manageable pieces, we are infused with the willpower to accomplish more with less stress.

I framed each chunk of tasks in order to relate it to my purpose by asking a simple question: "What is the right next move for me in this moment, as it relates to my purpose?" For example, if the tasks at hand in the "finance chunk" were to pay bills, consolidate credit cards, and shop around car insurance, I thought of these seemingly unrelated things as they related to my larger purpose — to be a presence and provider for Liam — and this helped to keep me motivated. Instead of just lying awake at night or sitting on my meditation cushion overwhelmed by the need to get my finances in order, I knew I could get there incrementally, and that each small task leaned in the same direction. As someone who hates to work out, I knew that improving my physical health by writing down something like "run three miles a day" would not work for me. But I discovered that by framing exercise as part of my larger purpose, and then writing down incremental goals — walk a block today, two blocks tomorrow, three blocks the next day, and so on — it became very doable.

It's not unlike how a rock climber scales a mountain. They don't do it by looking at or focusing on the summit. That would be intimidating and lead to failure. Instead, climbers break the climb into different segments, each manageable on its own, and all they think about is the next step, the next task at hand. Complete one step, then the next; finish one segment, then tackle another. Before you know it, you're at the top.

The night I did my "brain dump" and wrote down my tasks into chunks, my following meditation session was a success. I was less anxious and able to focus for short bursts on my breath, on expanding my heart, and on sending *metta* to other beings in my life. I felt more trust in myself and my abilities. After failure, it's perfectly natural to feel alone and to have a diminished sense of confidence. Self-doubt and insecurity are rampant, and the belief that we will not achieve our goals can become a self-fulfilling prophecy. On the contrary, when we pay attention to and track our small wins and milestones, we experience a boost of confidence and trust that we can keep going and complete the long, arduous road ahead. This can also become a self-fulfilling prophecy — a positive one.

When it comes to maintaining willpower, perception is everything; it can literally make or break our chance for success in reaching our goals or higher purpose. In a 2010 study conducted by Stanford University, researchers found that "people who believe they have an unlimited amount of willpower were able to work longer — without performing worse — than people who believe that they have only limited willpower." The experiment was conducted with university students who were given a test to take; those individuals who believed that willpower is a limited resource, otherwise known as limited resource theory, actually made more mistakes as the test went on. On the other hand, students who believed that willpower is an unlimited resource maintained their level of accuracy as the test went on. In short: If you believe that you have a limited amount of willpower, you're right! And if you believe you have an unlimited supply of willpower, you're right! To a large degree, we weave our own realities because our beliefs influence our actions. Taking action doesn't guarantee success — mountain climbers don't always summit — but often the limitations we put on ourselves are what hold us back.

In the days that followed, I was determined to use my circumstances and diagnosis to create a new narrative for myself, one that would transform my limitations into strengths. This wasn't easy. Whenever I leaned into fear and despair, my belief faltered, and I wasn't sure I had the willpower to make it through a normal day, let alone overcome all the obstacles ahead of me. When the feeling of hopelessness took over, it gobbled me up like quicksand. But then, like a ringing alarm disrupting a dream, I would take one look at Liam's big eyes and feel his grip around my neck when he embraced me, and I would remember how much he depended on me. When a three-year-old looks at you with hopeful eyes, it shapes the way you view yourself and what you believe you are capable of.

Identity shapes the way we view ourselves, which dictates our responses to emotional triggers and the narratives we use to explain the things we are good at or suck at. Our identities, narratives, and beliefs are most often based on our past experiences. During the lowest points in my life, they were times when I allowed myself to take on the identity of a victim, which inevitably resulted in the belief that I was disempowered and unable to change my life or situation. I was all too familiar with the pattern of victimhood spiraling into paralysis. Armed with pen and paper, and unconditional love for my son, I knew that the only thing standing in the way of shifting from paralysis to empowerment was one thing: me. I needed to work on shifting my identity, and that had to start with the stories I was telling myself.

Honestly, before I went through this, I would have rolled my eyes at that statement. It seems too simple and abstract. How can stories or the language we use have practical, concrete impact? But they do. I know from personal experience. Like the concept of chunking, flipping the script of your identity or revising your narrative is an incremental process. It's accomplished through thousands of small steps, not a single leap.

For example, imagine that someone is trying to quit smoking. Having smoked for years, they identify as a "smoker." That seems like a fact, but it's also a narrative, one that can hold them back. They might say that their doctor told them, to improve their health, "I am not allowed to smoke." Yet the phrase "I am not allowed" is from the perspective of someone who identifies as a smoker. Someone on a diet and who is trying to lose weight might say something similar: "I am not allowed to eat carbohydrates or fatty foods." This creates a sense of deprivation and gives away their power. By identifying as a smoker, the person can no longer do what defines them. Yet they can flip the script by saying, "I do not smoke." The implications are now reversed: They are a person who once chose to smoke and now chooses not to. Research has shown that this change in language can decrease feelings of deprivation and increase the amount of willpower it takes to quit smoking. This can empower us to reconstruct a new identity — that of someone who doesn't smoke.

In my case, I was walking around with the narrative: "I am a sickly, divorced, single mom who is going blind" — not exactly an inspiring identity. I knew I needed to flip the script, and so my new identity became: "I am a healthy, single mom who will inspire my son." Did I believe that narrative that evening? Not at all. A few weeks later? Not really. Months later? Somewhat. A year after that? Abso-fucking-lutely.

What changed? The *only* thing that changed overnight was my resolve to change my language, which paved the way for incremental shifts. I decided to try and consistently focus on high-level thinking instead of low-level thinking. The fundamental difference between the two is that low-level thinking focuses on *how* to complete a task, while high-level thinking focuses on *why*. An example of a low-level thought is, "How am I going to change my diet?" The answers to this question have to do with the process, short-term goals, and the execution. The high-level question, "Why do I want to change my diet?" is charged with purpose and meaning. When the going gets tough, this thinking can motivate us to summon the willpower to carry on.

Studies conducted by Professor Kentaro Fujita at Ohio State

University's School of Psychology have corroborated this. He and his colleagues have found that individuals who engage more frequently in high-level thinking have a higher amount of willpower, and also that perspectives, narratives, and thought patterns can be changed or revised; they are not set in stone. Simple shifts in the way people construe the world can have a direct effect on their willpower and self-control.

That said, in order to change the way we construe the world, we must first familiarize ourselves with how and why we view the world the way we do. In order to shift my way of thinking and remove the obstacles in my own path, I needed to understand *why* I was thinking in negative ways to begin with.

Leading Tibetan Buddhist scholar, meditation master, and monk Dzogchen Ponlop Rinpoche says that when we meditate we are both familiarizing our mind with our personal states or attitudes and with the mind itself and its true nature. This includes our entire attitude, approach, view, perspective, and deeper understanding of ourselves. What I learned through this process, and where I think many people get stuck, is that the mind is not merely the thinking or reasoning process. The mind is our experience, too. It is our reality. When we speak of transforming our mind, cultivating our mind, or developing our mind, we are talking about transforming our reality. The practice of meditation transforms our whole reality, our entire way of perceiving and responding. I realize now that when I was sitting on that cushion, I was transforming my reality with wisdom, curiosity, insight, compassion, joy, and kindness. Only then could I understand my mind's true nature, reality's true nature, and see who and what I am. Having this information provided me with the willpower to create and sustain the shifts I longed for.

CHAPTER FIVE

Sustainable Self-Care

I have come to believe that caring for myself is not self-indulgent.
Caring for myself is an act of survival.

— AUDRE LORDE

After two weeks of my new morning and evening rituals —
journaling and meditation — I had my appointment at the
rheumatologist's office for my first infusion of Humira. At the
time, this was a fairly new-to-the-market immunosuppressive
drug, one that blocks a specific immune antibody that causes
inflammation. It is used to treat autoimmune conditions like ar-
thritis, plaque psoriasis, Crohn's disease, and ankylosing spondylitis — the disease I was suspected to have, which my doctor
believed was causing my uveitis flare-ups. Like chemotherapy, the
drug is administered intravenously for several hours through a
drip. Accompanied by my mother and my friend Gilda, I arrived
at Mount Sinai Medical Center on a sunny, clear day in Miami
Beach. We brought magazines, snacks, and DVDs of feel-good

"chick flicks," as well as a positive attitude about the process and the outcome.

The nurse took us into a small room in the back used exclusively for infusions. Someone had obviously tried really hard to make the room look warm and inviting with the color scheme, but it still managed to feel clinical and sterile. My eyes immediately gravitated toward the window facing east, affording me a distant view of the Atlantic Ocean. The nurse took my vitals and blood samples, reviewed all my paperwork, and inserted the intravenous tube into my left arm. Moments later the doctor arrived, chatted with us and made me feel at ease, and then gave the nurse the instructions to start the drip. I felt a slight burn in my vein as the cool liquid entered my body, but it was manageable. I asked Gilda to get the movie going, and as she dug through the bag looking for the DVD, I closed my eyes and started chanting to myself: *I am not broken.... I am healed.... I am not broken.... I am healed....*

When the movie's symphonic opening theme began, I opened my eyes and happily watched, feeling supported on a beautiful sunny day. I honestly felt like I was "on my way." Then after about ten minutes, I started to feel an itchiness throughout my body, followed by a scratchy feeling in my throat. I tried to ignore it at first, but with each second it became more and more pronounced. I turned to my mother, who was watching the mounted television screen, and said, "I feel itchy." When she looked at me, her eyes widened and she yelled, "Oh my God! You are so red and swollen!"

Gilda ran out of the room to call the nurse. At that moment, I started to panic: My heart was pounding through my chest, I could feel my blood pressure dropping, and my throat was closing up. The nurse took one look at me, shoved my mom aside, called into the hallway for backup, and immediately disconnected the drip bag. She looked me straight in the eyes and asked me to speak, but I could not vocalize any sound. I could barely breathe; it felt like I was being held underwater. I was going into anaphylactic shock. A second nurse rushed in with an autoinjector device (I later learned it contained epinephrine), and immediately stabbed me in the thigh. Within moments, my blood pressure stabilized and my airways opened again. Meanwhile, my doctor arrived and spoke to my mother, but I only caught snippets of what he said: "allergic reaction... another drug option available... get some rest."

I left the hospital that day feeling like a failure. Every cell in my body was failing me, and somehow, I reasoned, it was my fault. All the positive thinking and willpower I had been working on for weeks was thrown out the window. That evening, after Liam was asleep, and after my mom left, I reluctantly turned to my meditation cushion. I was ready to come undone. As soon as I sat down, I sobbed uncontrollably, and when I had no more tears left, I settled down and fell back, lying flat on the floor. I must have fallen asleep because at close to 5 a.m. I was woken up by my yellow Labrador, who rested his head on my chest. I laid there, stroking his fur, staring at the ceiling for a few moments, realizing that, at least for now, I could see the ceiling.

Stress Is Not Always a Bad Thing

Have you ever pruned or cut back a tree or a plant, then been shocked at how barren it looks? Only to then watch with amazement as each branch explodes with new life? I used to be reluctant to cut back any plant until someone told me that it is actually good for plants. It goes against everything that we think is "healthy."

How could inflicting such trauma and stress help plants grow and, yes, even thrive? This is just a simple example of nature's fight for survival. When we prune the plant or tree, it then puts even greater energy into growing more. Having been hacked to pieces, plants and trees could decide to give in, to just shrivel up and die. But they don't. The same is true for us. When things get tough, we can choose to give in or to give more, to get bitter or to get better. We can choose to mirror nature and face our problems rather than run from them. We can choose to meet the stressors we are facing and use them to help us expand our capacity for resilience and perhaps even thrive as a result.

That morning while lying on the floor, as scared as I was about the future, I thought about the blessings of this curse. I thought about Mary Oliver's poem "The Uses of Sorrow": "Someone I loved once gave me a box full of darkness. It took me years to understand that this, too, was a gift." In my box full of darkness were the fossilized remains of a failed marriage, but I also had my son. My physical body was failing me, but it was also asking me to take note and remember to appreciate my health. My mental condition was frightening me, but it also presented an opportunity for me to step into courage. My life had been dictated for so long by other people and forces — my parents, my husband, my religion, societal norms — and now I was free to make my own decision. This was *my* reckoning to choose, and I was consciously going to lean into it. I knew that change is one of the only certain things in our lives, and so I had that choice to make. I wanted to get better, and I knew that required me to give more. I wanted to try and accept this box of darkness and see it as a positive thing, a gift, as much as possible.

I sat up slowly. My dog was not ready to get up; he just rolled his head to the other side and continued to sleep. I walked into the kitchen to make myself a cup of coffee, and as the coffee machine was heating up the water, I saw my first decision point out of the corner of my eye. On the kitchen table, with a pencil as a placeholder between the pages, was my bright red journal, staring at me, perhaps even taunting me. *Do the work*, it whispered. I sat down, placed my warm mug to the left of me, and opened up the journal to a fresh page. I made a list of all the things I could explore to try and get healthy. I didn't want to try another medication. My body was telling me something, leading me in a different direction — this I knew for sure.

My numbered list was just a free flow of all the things I knew were good for me, things like acupuncture, yoga, an anti-inflammatory diet, the beach, fresh air, meditation, girl time, me time, and long walks, to name a few. I also added other coping mechanisms, like saying no, asserting myself, and managing my time. Then, as I had before with my enormous to-do list, I chunked the information into what seemed like five natural categories:

- Work/professional
- Physical/fitness
- Emotional/mind
- Spiritual
- Relationships/community

Each category listed strategies or activities I enjoy that also would contribute to my well-being, items that were completely authentic to me. Some of these categories started to intersect, and I later learned that this is perfectly normal.

Sample Category: Emotional Self-Care

- Journal daily
- Meditate at least once daily for twenty minutes
- Develop/cultivate friendships that are supportive
- Do one outdoor pleasurable activity at least once a week
- Allow myself to safely experience my full range of emotions; identify them
- Meet socially with a support group/friends at least once a week
- Schedule time to DO NOTHING

Feeling satisfied with my progress that morning, I put my mug in the sink, went upstairs to wake Liam and get him to school, and start my workday. I resolved to tackle a couple of things in my physical/fitness category during my break — like make an appointment for acupuncture and research foods that help reduce inflammation in autoimmune conditions. I didn't know it then, but by memorializing my wellness strategies, I was actually putting together a formal self-care plan, also known as a coping plan.

The Importance of Authentic Self-Care

Before exploring further the enormous impact this made in my life, I want to discuss self-care in general: what it is, what it isn't, why we need it, and how a self-care plan can help us on the path to "better."

Self-care means we commit to taking an active role in safeguarding our mental and physical wellness, proactively and (especially) in times of duress.

By definition, self-care means doing what is good for us — increasing our emotional and physical stamina, improving our self-esteem, and building resilience. Maintaining good self-care ensures that we stay compassionate, impassioned, and engaged. It means doing important work in one area without sacrificing other parts of our life. It means maintaining a positive attitude in spite of personal challenges and the larger injustices in the world. Self-care activities create daily improvement in our lives and have beneficial long-term effects. That said, these activities are not always fun. Sometimes they even border on boring.

We also might feel guilty about self-care because it can go against what we've been taught, which is that to be a good friend, parent, spouse or partner, coworker, and community member we have to put others first. Self-care means putting ourselves first, and we're often conditioned to believe this is wrong. It's rude. It isn't consistent with how so many inspirational leaders throughout history are portrayed, such as Gandhi, Nelson Mandela, Martin Luther King Jr., Susan B. Anthony, and Margaret Sanger. We admire these individuals because they endured suffering and hardship and practiced self-sacrifice. Proper nutrition, healthy relationships, and exercise are secondary, if not frivolous. They didn't have time for yoga!

Two problems contribute to a negative view of self-care. The first issue is what I mention above, that self-care is often considered self-centered. It can imply caring that extends only to ourselves as individuals. But we can expand our definition of *self* to extend beyond the individual and include our family, community, the natural world, and all sentient beings. Self-care actually means caring for the entire community of which we are a part; it encompasses and protects this larger order. Self-care is not about being virtuous. In a way, it means living and working in ways that are consistent with and model how we want the world to work.

The second issue is that the concept of self-care has been hijacked by corporations to create a very profitable industrial wellness complex, one that focuses on beauty, happiness, and comfort in the name of self-love and self-compassion. In Western society, this is mostly geared toward white women of means, but it can include anyone. The main goal of this industry is to sell goods and services that provide only a superficial appearance of self-care, one that is often, in fact, indulgent and frivolous precisely because it's a temporary quick fix that only aims to make the individual feel better about themselves.

The reality is that authentic self-care is unsexy, hard work — which isn't an attractive marketing pitch for corporations or brands. The way the term is broadly used today has very little to do with the healthy choices that reflect true self-love and self-compassion. It certainly has nothing to do with the struggle to survive in the face of political and structural oppression. For communities that are under attack by their own government, and for individuals with little access to health care, fresh food, clean water, and safe housing, self-care is a radical act of self-preservation. Authentic self-care is for everyone. It's what we all need and deserve, but it can be hard because it's not a quick fix. Ironically, neither is our own inner journey, or something as lofty as social justice work. Seen this way, wellness is one aspect of social justice, and like social justice, wellness doesn't happen overnight. This is another reason that self-care has gotten such a bad name: It is much easier to practice "self-care" in easy ways that feel good right now than it is to develop the discipline of a healthy lifestyle that often sucks in the moment but feels really great later. Authentic self-care

is not self-indulgence. Self-indulgence is unrestrained gratifica-
tion of our desires and whims, behaviors meant only to alter our
mood and provide a temporary escape from pain and grief.

How can we tell the difference between self-indulgence and
true acts of self-care? First, ask if what you're doing is a temporary
quick fix or something that is meant to yield long-term benefits.
Sometimes, self-care is best expressed by setting limits in ways
that prioritize what's most important. This takes discipline. Some
everyday examples might include watching only one episode of a
TV show, not binging a whole season, so you get to bed at a decent
hour and experience a full night's rest. It might be not having a
glass of wine with dinner, or only having one; saying no when you
don't want to do something; or waking up early so you have extra
time to meditate, journal, or exercise before work.

The morning when I wrote my own self-care list, which was
my response to true despair and a will to survive, I felt an in-
stinctual inner knowing that I had to give up most of my vices in
order to truly dedicate myself to self-care, to my healing, and to
my overall wellness. If the work we do in the world is larger than
ourselves — and for me at that moment being a mother to my
son was just that — then self-care means defining clear boundaries that help ensure our long-term physical, mental, and spiritual
health. But I didn't give up *all* my vices. I knew there were healthy
indulgences I could still enjoy, ones that provided important moments of joy and happiness. For me, these were defined by even
the smallest of actions that helped me restore balance during one
of the most imbalanced periods in my life. This included things
like spending an evening reading a good book with a mud mask
on my face; shutting down my phone and not responding to texts
or emails for a few hours of solitude; and having a meal with a

friend while engaging in meaningful conversation. I didn't consider any of these things frivolous.

My point is this: Self-care is not one-size-fits-all. We each must decide what's right for ourselves. The biggest challenge I needed to overcome was the guilt and ingrained belief that taking *any* time for myself was selfish. In the end, what I learned from this experience is that tending to myself is a way to reaffirm that I value myself, and because I do, I must also honor myself. Taking that time to reaffirm in writing that "I am not broken" set me on my path and positioned me front and center as my own cheerleader and self-advocate. Yet I can also proclaim irrefutably that authentic self-care is a truly selfless act — one that made me into a healthier being, a more engaged mother, and eventually, an impassioned self-care activist.

CHAPTER SIX

Kindsight

*View your life with kindsight. Stop beating yourself up
about things from your past. Instead of slapping your forehead
and asking, "What was I thinking," breathe and ask yourself
the kinder question, "What was I learning."*

— KAREN SALMANSOHN

A week after my allergic reaction to the infusion, I went back to see my ophthalmologist for a follow-up appointment. She was content with the stability in my eyesight from the steroid injection, but she was not happy to hear about the severity of my experience. "I really don't think you have ankylosing spondylitis, anyway," she said nonchalantly, as she examined my eyes through a loupe while shining a bright light into my pupils. "The way your eye disease is manifesting itself is inconsistent with what I've seen in patients with AS. The shots seem to be working, so we will just do that for as long as we can and see where that gets us."

As she said that, I felt an immediate rush of blood through my body straight up to my head — it felt like I had been forced underwater and was finally coming up and getting some air. I glommed on to her opinion like syrup poured on pancakes. I didn't care if it needed to be more fully vetted or investigated. As far as I was concerned, it was case closed. Her words gave me the gift of possibility, which I needed in order to truly believe that I could heal. Up until then, I had only hoped I could heal. I thought *only* going blind would be a blessing. Now, with those words, the possibility that my spine would not calcify into one bone and immobilize me, that I would not end up in a wheelchair, that I would not be a burden to others became real. An independent life became attainable again. The possibility of a return to "me" — even if it was a different version of me — was a gift.

In 1902, the philosopher William James, who helped establish psychology as a formal discipline, wrote in *The Varieties of Religious Experience* that there are two kinds of people: the "once-born" and "twice-born." Once-born people are biologically predisposed to happiness. These individuals have an almost childlike acceptance of the way life is; they aren't bothered by the intense suffering or evil in the world. Yet should these individuals find themselves in a traumatic event or crisis, they don't use the opportunity to grow and expand. Instead, they remain in the dark place, stunted by the experience, never wandering too far from the safety of who they thought they were. Conversely, twice-born people use personal adversity and setbacks as opportunities for an inner reckoning, an opportunity to become the better (or best) version of themselves. These individuals look for purpose and meaning in these dark moments. The darkness becomes an invitation to live more consciously and to seek out the light that remains, even if it is hidden from plain view.

James posits that people who are twice-born are happier because, when they come out on the other side of the crisis, they have made more sense of the universe (or at least of their own lives), and they have a much greater appreciation for their life and the world. He writes that "the process is one of redemption, not of mere reversion to natural health, and the sufferer, when saved, is saved by what seems to him a second birth, a deeper kind of conscious being than he could enjoy before." Confucius put this another way: "We all have two lives; the second one begins when we realize we only have one." Personally, when I came out of literal darkness, this was the impetus for me to ask *why* and *how* I had entered a despairing and bleak space to begin with. Though I didn't relate to the religious implications, I felt renewed and "born again," similar to any experience where there is a trauma, a near-death experience, or a severe illness followed by an awakening.

An awakening of this magnitude has stages similar to the process of grief — denial, anger, bargaining, depression, and acceptance. We go through a loss, a loss that can be ambiguous and unclear, lacking a defined resolution. It can be physical, such as my loss of eyesight, or something more drastic, like a missing person. But it can also be more psychological, like when we "lose" a family member to dementia or a serious addiction, or when a partner cheats and we realize our relationship can never go back to the way it was. For me, I experienced the convergence of so many losses — my marriage, my home, my family unit, my health, the future as I had envisioned it, my way of life. Whatever occurs, we find ourselves on an uncharted path.

I was trained, like many in Western culture, to be driven, goal-oriented, and always seeking definitive solutions. This attitude or approach is certainly a double-edged sword. On the one hand, it's the reason I strove to graduate high school at the age of fifteen and become the president of a midsize company by the age of thirty-six. On the other hand, I found this way of thinking utterly destructive when I was faced with a problem that had no solution — or none that I was pleased with. I discovered that a true awakening means committing to the radical acceptance that there may not be a solution, that certain things may not be under my control and may never be, and that I need to stop looking at my life with regret-filled hindsight. Instead, I needed kindsight.

I liken the concept of radical acceptance to the children's board game Chutes and Ladders. The game has a hundred squares, and randomly placed among them are ladders that boost you forward, so that you skip some number of squares, and chutes or slides that send you backward to a lower square. The worst place to land on the board is on the eighty-seventh square, just thirteen squares short of winning the game. On that square is a slide that sends you all the way back to the twenty-fourth square — basically, almost back to the beginning. Thus, players never know what will happen. With one spin of the wheel, the player in the lead could fall to last, and a player in the middle might jump to the front. Just like life. When we land on a slide, we tend to think life is being "unfair," but life isn't unfair. At some point, *everyone* hits a slide, and the ride down can be hard to stomach. Having radical acceptance means accepting whatever square we land on as the new baseline from which we must continue climbing. Blindness was my new baseline.

In other words, radical acceptance is not the same as giving up. If we land on a slide, we don't quit the game. Instead, it means no longer resisting or fighting reality; rather, we apply our energies to moving forward again. Doing this allowed me to clear the mental space I needed to be constructive and proactive, instead of keeping me mired in a state of self-torment. However, acceptance can only happen through forgiveness. A trusted friend who is a psychotherapist once told me that we all walk around as two versions of ourselves. We have a version of ourselves that is the unconditioned self — innocent, untouched by any trauma, criticism, or injustice we may have faced in our lives. The other version is the learned self, which we commonly refer to as the ego, which works hard to separate us from the truth of who we really are — human beings who are whole and healthy. What does the ego focus on? Everything that is perceived as good on the "outside" — achievements, things that are praiseworthy and yield dividends.

The morning after my ophthalmologist suggested I might not have ankylosing spondylitis, my unconditioned self showed up. It knew that I was already the person I wanted to be and that I just had to show up in the world and for myself the way I was, flaws, fractures, and all. All the happiness I had been seeking on the outside — being the perpetual people pleaser, protecting my image of the "perfect" self — had led me to darkness. When we are stopped in our tracks, we stop chasing and can start choosing. Choosing forgiveness is the first step. By reflecting on our past with kindsight, we can forgive ourselves for all the times we allowed the ego to block our authenticity. But kindsight doesn't only apply to the past, and that's a good thing — because we actually live in the present, and we need to bring compassion and kindness to the now as well.

Finding Our Self-Care Rhythms

Life is a sequence of high points and low points. Rarely, if ever, is our path from one point to another a straight line. Rather, when we track the rhythm of our life, it's a sequence of zigzags or peaks and valleys. Reminiscent of a heartbeat monitor, this pattern indicates that we are very much alive. On that monitor, and in life, we aren't seeking a flat line. We strive to be grateful for the peaks, graceful in the valleys, and content on the plateaus. Sustainable self-care follows this same cadence.

What does a sustainable self-care regimen look like? It doesn't look like a list of New Year's resolutions. Most of those never get kept. Just because I wrote down a list of things that I knew should be the cornerstone of my "self-care plan" didn't mean I suddenly enacted everything without fail from then on. I failed miserably, in fact. Following through was incredibly difficult. There were days I didn't seek support or get exercise; days when I ate and drank things I knew would increase my inflammation. I didn't always create healthy boundaries with others. Oftentimes I took on more than I should have. My lingering guilt over being a single mom and my need to please people in order to amplify my self-worth didn't vanish. Eventually, though, by not beating myself up for these infractions and by giving myself permission to begin anew each day — coupled with putting in place the most critical component of all, a community of care — I was able to develop a self-care rhythm.

Through this trial and error, I learned that, to be sustainable, a self-care plan needs to be gentle enough to work. It has to be incremental and composed of a lot of little things. Self-care might start as a set of promises we make to ourselves, but to enact them, we need to find a rhythm we can live with. Like a musical rhythm, a self-care rhythm is a regular, repeated pattern of actions that helps maintain the song of our life. That is, this rhythm is integrated into and supports whatever we are already doing on a daily basis. It's not a disruption. Rather, it enhances our life. There are actually four self-care rhythms we can focus on: daily, weekly, seasonally, and annually.

Getting into a new self-care groove wasn't easy at first. Like most people, I have a hard time creating and maintaining a balance between work, social life, family, and other obligations. Every evening and on the weekends, I would take my work home with me, whether it was task-related work (such as paperwork or answering emails) or emotional work (bearing the burdens of my community or clients). Of course, I couldn't entirely stop bringing work home at times (who can?), but I needed to establish a more formal separation between work and my personal space.

One of the ways that helped me create a better work-life balance was to identify the mudrooms in my life, so to speak. Just like a home's entryway, I developed formal transition rituals or practices that allowed me to shift from my public self to my personal self. Over time, these micropractices became healthy habits that contributed to my overall self-care. For example, on my commute home, I practiced mindful driving in silence instead of taking phone calls or listening to talk radio. As soon as I got home from work, I took a walk around the block — with the dog and without my phone! After arriving somewhere, I sat in my parked car for a few moments and took the time to do a quick breathing exercise, then set an intention before rushing into the house or into my son's preschool. These seemingly small things allowed me to let go of the stressors from work and to show up more fully present in the other areas of my life. Like a mudroom, they helped me wash off the proverbial mud from my shoes, so I could move into the next activity without tracking emotional dirt from my previous activity. These became integral parts of my daily self-care practice.

To achieve a weekly rhythm, I wanted to balance my activities between four different areas that I identified: work, family and relationships, "me time," and my cultural traditions. Every week, I tried to be conscious about making sure that each of these areas was getting enough of my time and that they were balanced in ways that provided me energy and nourishment. Then, I looked at longer stretches of time and considered each season and each year and asked: Was I providing for all my needs on a regular, ongoing basis? This took careful scrutiny and constant adjustment. Not every day, week, season, or year is the same, and I never found a perfect balance or formula that worked all the time.

Cleaning Up the Clutter

Consider the rhythms of your daily life — what would qualify as your mudrooms? What physical spaces or natural pauses already exist that would allow you to transition more elegantly from one demand or obligation to another? What about the weekly balance of your activities? Are some areas of your life being overrun or overwhelmed by others? You are the architect of your life, so consider your whole house and how to change things so that you can function at your best.

As you do this, one thing you might realize is that your home could be nice and fulfilling to live in if it weren't so full of clutter, if it weren't in such disarray. Every home has a junk drawer or two, along with a hallway closet or room where we hide our clutter when guests come over. We may fool our guests, but the clutter remains once they leave, and it inevitably spills over and grows. Mudrooms are like magnets for clutter — full of carelessly strewn shoes and boots, rain jackets and winter coats, single gloves without a matching pair, duffel bags filled with equipment and uniforms, and even bags of new but unused items that, despite our good intentions, are still waiting to be returned to the store even after months and months. The problem with this chaotic scene is that the mayhem eventually becomes an obstacle, a literal physical boundary preventing us from entering our home — or exiting, for that matter. Before leaving the house, we waste time pawing through this minefield looking for the "other" shoe or that matching glove. What can undo this madness? A team effort, of course. We need to take a community approach to the common cause of self-care.

Despite my efforts and best-laid plans — despite writing down and chunking my self-care activities, despite focusing on mudrooms and building smaller habits — I still consistently fell short of meeting my goals. I couldn't adhere to my self-care plan because I was constantly tripping over my own clutter. Eventually, all the women in my life who had become my support system were the ones who helped me get this mess in order. These women were friends who became sisters; some were only acquaintances when I was married but became my safety net once I was a single mom. Ultimately, this group of individuals became my formal "community of care," and they were exactly what I needed in order to fulfill my obligations to myself.

My friend Helen helped me realize this epiphany one day as I was venting to her about how I had no time or energy left at the end of every night to take care of even one thing on the list. She asked me a simple, direct question: "What do you need right now in order to get one thing done?" That question stopped me in my tracks because I couldn't remember the last time anybody had asked me what *I needed*. Helen, a savvy and sharp business executive and fellow mom whom I had befriended through our sons' after-school karate classes, cut through my dumbstruck silence and asked again: "What do you need *right now* to get to one thing on your list on a regular basis? Be specific."

"I need more time in the mornings. I need someone to take Liam to school some mornings. That would give me time to do yoga, exercise, journal, or even meal plan," I responded.

"Great. That's perfect." Helen sprang into action, as she normally did. She told me not to worry, that she was "handling" things, and within hours, she had arranged for a school-morning carpool plan with her, her next-door neighbor, and me. Suddenly, after loading Liam into the car with his backpack and lunchbox, I had close to a full hour available to me twice a week. For a single mom with chronic health issues, this was a huge gift. Years later, I was able to return the favor and do the same for another single mom.

After this intervention from Helen, I spent one of my treasured hours reflecting on my self-care list again. I rewrote the list, dedicating a single page to each self-care category. I created three columns on each page; in one column I listed each activity in that category, and in the second column I wrote down obstacles. I identified each shoe and piece of clutter in my mudrooms. I asked what was getting in the way of partaking in each activity, writing down things like time, finances, and skills. Then, in the third column, I strategized ways to remove these barriers, listing things either I could do or someone else might do for me.

Three key things emerged for me during this process: First, I realized that I needed the support of a friend or community to be able to remove many of these obstacles. Second, I understood that there were self-care items where I was, in fact, the only obstacle, since they involved issues like motivation, discipline, and self-esteem, to name a few. For these, by taking a good, hard, realistic look at myself, I realized that I needed someone to hold me accountable when I would not hold myself accountable. Lastly, I realized that some of the items on my list were too ambitious and unrealistic for where I was, and I gave myself permission to remove those items or to leave my plan open for adjustment over time. My self-care plan was not written in stone. It was a living, breathing document that would change over time, as my life and demands changed. It was a document that depended on the support of an entire community.

Not only that, I soon helped everyone in that community formulate their own self-care plans. In time, we would weave together a mutually beneficial safety net of care and support that ensured we could all obtain what we needed, ask for help without guilt, remove obstacles from our path of self-preservation, and hold one another accountable with love and with kindsight.

PART TWO

SHOW UP

[The Outer Journey to We]

CHAPTER SEVEN

Where Is Our Village?

In and through community lies the salvation of the world.

— M. Scott Peck

O ne Thursday evening, when Liam was spending the night at his father's house, I invited over the women who had showed up for me in the months leading up to my divorce, during my health scares, and as I was trying to get into the new single mom groove. It was a gathering of a new sisterhood, as I saw it. Some of the women knew one another, some were no more than acquaintances at the beginning of my journey but had become more than family in a matter of months, and some I'd known for almost the entirety of my life. All of us were mothers. I knew we could all use some time away from our children and families to decompress and just enjoy some laughs and a glass or two of wine, but I also knew that we could greatly benefit from a meaningful experience together, one that would help weave a safety net for all of us. What

I didn't know is how this community of care would become my fire when I could not feel my own flames.

After my epiphany with Helen, I realized how isolating my self-care plan up to then had been. It didn't weave in accountability or leave room for support. However, I also soon found that asking for help consistently is hard, especially as you rotate requests among the people in your phone book and have to conduct a cost-benefit analysis before every call. To achieve sustainable self-care, I needed a sustainable community of care, so I selfishly brought these women together that evening to hopefully create that. I wanted to move away from individual self-care. I didn't want to heal on my own. I wasn't cut out for it. I wanted a built-in safety net, a formal community I could turn to and share my self-care plan with, discuss my obstacles, and ask for help to find tangible solutions. Knowing my own limitations as a human being, I wanted to have a network of individuals surrounding me who could hold me accountable and keep me to my own word. Perhaps most importantly, I also wanted to offer this same help to the women helping me.

As we all gathered in the tight space of my living room and spilled into the dining area, I "ahemed" loudly, garnering everyone's attention. With all eyes on me, I took a deep breath, my heart practically leaping out of my chest, and I said three words I never thought I would utter out loud before a group: "I need help." Some eyes widened in surprise, but every person leaned in further and moved closer into the circle. After a pause, I continued, "I think that my plea for help may actually be able to help all of us. As they say, a rising tide lifts all ships." Then I reviewed my situation, filling in the blanks for some of the attendees who were not familiar with the extent of my health issues, my financial woes, and my struggles on a daily basis. I talked about the journey that had led me to write down my coping plan, and I took out the self-care plan I had put together for myself to show them the extent of my thought process.

I outlined where I was struggling the most, why I believed I was failing to succeed in clawing my way back to a semblance of health, and how I was losing hope that I would ever find balance. "We always hear that it takes a village to raise a child," I said, "but where is *our* village? I need a village of my own, too." I told this gathering of sisters about how I had learned the hard way during the darkest moments of the last few months that our culture's value system actually rejects the collective responsibility that we have for one another's well-being. I told them how difficult it was to put myself first and to keep my promises to myself. Every single head in the room nodded in consensus. "Listen, none of us lives in a vacuum. We are all connected, right? These connections are real. It's why you're here. So even though it's easy for us to feel isolated in this increasingly electronic and technology-based world, the village philosophy of our ancestors still rings true. I want to reclaim that philosophy. This is why I brought you here tonight. I want to create a formal community of care. I don't want to merely survive — I need to thrive. I can't do it alone. None of us can."

That evening, my words were met with so much support. My sisterhood moved all their chips into the center of the table; they were "all in." My words wielded a sledgehammer to the invisible but very real walls that were separating each of us. That evening was about a new order — coexistence. We affirmed that, while each of us is whole and self-sufficient, together we could be a community. And community is everything. Our desire, our need, and our responsibility to take care of one another are just as valid as the task of taking care of ourselves. Community care is part of self-care and just as vital to our individual wellness, growth, and forward movement.

Independence Is a Myth

Close your eyes for a moment and feel this book in your hands (or imagine you are holding a book). As you do, think about all the people it took to create this one, singular book. People planted the trees that were grown to make the paper, others cut down the trees and transported them to the lumberyard, and others at the paper mill processed the pulp necessary to make the paper. Whole teams of people designed and built the machinery used during each step of manufacturing, and still others produced the energy that powered the paper mill, whether that involved drilling for oil, mining coal, or building solar panels. Other individuals made the ink and dyes used to print the text; others designed the cover and the interiors; and still more people edited, typeset, proofread, printed, packaged, shipped, and sold the book.

This book has one author, me. But I didn't write this alone. Thousands of individuals have touched my life and influenced what I've written; I've been shaped and educated by their thoughts and deeds, which have impacted how I express myself and what I want to communicate. And the same is true for every single book in your home, for every book in your town's library, for every book in the world. The circles expand even further. Consider that no one who helped create this book could have survived without others to harvest and produce the food they consumed, to build the cars and trains they rode, to teach and care for their children while they were at work. And none of us would be here at all if it wasn't for our parents, grandparents, great-grandparents, and so on. No one would exist without those who came before and gave of themselves and sacrificed to ensure that we were born. In the end, not only every book but every person who exists is interconnected.

To think that any individual could be completely independent is laughable. There is no such thing as true independence. So, as you read, think about the fact that, in a very real sense, this book is a gift to you from the whole world, past and present. The story of a physical book — as much as the words written in the book — dates back to the birth of this planet — and beyond. It is a truly amazing thing to ponder just how interconnected we are. I often pause to bless my food or a glass of wine or juice, to ponder the origins of a new sweater, or to marvel at a grand sculpture or building. I think about the millions of hands that directly and indirectly contributed to each of these things, and I am filled with gratitude. This isn't just about the individuals; I consider the communities that surrounded and supported them so that each person could create, contribute, and in some cases simply exist. The necessities of life rarely come from one's own hands, but rather from a complicated "web of mutuality," as Martin Luther King Jr. phrased it.

The human need for community goes well beyond mere survival. Of course, people rely on community for life's necessities, but most people want to be part of a community to feel less lonely, for joy, companionship, and love. There is something indescribably lovely about being part of a group of people who share a sense of purpose, camaraderie, and belonging. Community helps us not just survive but thrive. I remember hearing Hillary Clinton, when she was the First Lady, speak while on tour for her book *It Takes a Village*. She said that a lot of people were confused about the title and would ask her, "What the heck do you mean by that?" She would respond, "None of us can raise a family, build a business, or heal a community... totally alone." I remember hearing her saying those words but not completely understanding how much I would need a community at a time in my life when I felt no fire. The Sufi tradition teaches that the primary purpose of life is to awaken to the essence of who we are, which is likened to lighting a fire within. Once we do, we are invited to lovingly embrace this realization of our essence. The gift of community is that it offers each of us the fire of affirmation and support to achieve this and to keep the fire going, even on the days when we feel no fire. When I gathered my sisterhood, my embers were starting to fade with each passing day, and I found it increasingly difficult to fan my own flames — the flames that were required to warm another human being in my care.

Communities of Care: A New Order

There is an anecdote told about a famous Irish storyteller named Peig Sayers who once lived in the Blasket Islands off the coast of Ireland. The winds are so great that even trees can't survive on this island, and she was asked, "How can you live in a place like this?" To which she responded quite simply, "It is in the shelter of each other that the people live."

In the West, self-care almost always focuses on the individual and on what we can do for ourselves. We're taught that each individual has all they need, that the power for transformation and thriving lies within, just waiting to be harnessed. We are taught not to be a burden on others, and that we alone should beat back the demons plaguing us and come through to the other side refreshed and ready to fight again. My sisterhood affirmed the opposite that evening. They agreed that to do everything my self-care plan called for would be impossible for any single person. They affirmed that sometimes even doing one thing for oneself can feel impossible. My friend Suzanne said it best when she remarked, "We live in a culture that demonizes the burdensome, and so for that reason alone it feels almost unthinkable for most of us to reach out and ask for help."

That evening, we began to put together the pieces of the puzzle and to create a formalized community of care. We discussed all the logistics of how often we should meet, what "templates" we could all work on and share with one another as we reflected on our own self-care needs, our obstacles and barriers, and how we could tangibly help one another — by lifting one another up, calling one another out, and making it easier to ask for help. Someone pointed out that we needed to make it easier not to have to ask for help in the first place. Having a community doesn't mean only asking "what can you do for me" but also "what can I do for you." We had to figure out a way to build mutually beneficial relationships between us, which meant balancing the desire and expectation to receive care from others with the commitment to provide and administer care to others.

Caring for ourselves can — and should — be done together. That seems like such a natural and simple notion, so why are there so many issues with formally forming a community of care? Sometimes we may feel overworked, and when this happens, we often turn inward. Our jobs don't stop, and we often can't stop. We may assume others are too stressed to be able to provide support, and asking for support can be humbling or embarrassing. Further, it's hard enough to make new friends at any age, but I keep hearing from women over fifty that it's especially hard, if not downright impossible, as you get older.

We left that evening with some homework, a date for our next gathering, and a few prompts to think about. We agreed to spend time considering what type of support we would need from an ideal community of care in order to be able to be the best version of ourselves — which meant a version of ourselves that could continue to give back. We had to be willing to truthfully describe the obstacles or hang-ups that we would personally need to overcome. At that time, here is what I wrote about my vision for what an ideal community of care would look like:

> I have a strong, tight-knit community of caring folks that holds me when I can't hold myself. I have a network of people that check in on me when they realize I'm in the sunken place instead of waiting for me to reach out because I probably won't. They help me figure out what my needs are, and take care of them for me. Friends and comrades feed me, donate their old linens and bath towels, maybe even furniture. They gift me with bath bombs and tea and maybe even time, by taking care of my son for a few hours. I didn't always want to ask for help. I wanted it to be offered to me. I wanted people to proactively show up sometimes. I wanted to be able to do the same for others so that I could feel worthy and fulfilled, too.

One thing that our community agreed on was that people don't always just "show up." We knew that we needed to destigmatize burdening others and normalize asking for help. We wanted it inherently understood that being part of this group meant doing both. What true community care eventually came to symbolize for us was a liberation of sorts. For those of us who were managing and struggling alone, fearing the burden we would place on others, it meant we could rely on receiving the support that we needed. In my case, support as I fought for my health, support that kept me alive. More generally, it meant that when someone said they were going through something tough, we wouldn't respond by just offering advice, telling them what they could do for themselves, or reminding them to "take care of yourself." Instead, to the extent that we could, we would ask, "How can I support you?" None of these women asked me, as a single mother, if I was taking care of myself without also offering some way to help me do so. It meant that if someone lost a job, and with it the ability to take care of their family, we wouldn't just ask, "How's the job search going?" We offered to open doors and make introductions that might lead to a new job. We actively helped that person figure out how to get their children fed and keep a roof over their head.

For me personally, I recognized my own tendency to detach when I needed support the most, so this aspect of our community of care became essential. The structure didn't allow for my isolation or my detachment because we all agreed to accept a collective responsibility to one another. By both caring for others and in turn being cared for, we were able to collectively heal. My sisters' healing was bound in my own healing, and vice versa.

This may sound entirely utopian — to think that such a community could exist, that one could feel truly held and seen without feeling guilt, or that being a part of such a deliberately woven web wouldn't be experienced as a burden. Yet it isn't utopian at all. It's such a natural way for humans to coexist, support, and elevate one another. It's the way we have operated since the dawn of humankind. The largest obstacle to overcome is getting the ball rolling. At least one individual must be courageous enough to approach others and invite the conversation. If I had waited for the conversation to evolve naturally, it likely would not have happened. Approaching others with this vision was nerve-racking for me in very much the same way as asking someone out on a first date. The fear of rejection was very palpable, but I can reassure you that the rewards outweigh the risk.

If this concept speaks to you, be the person who gets the ball rolling. Invite a group of people to meet one afternoon in much the same way that you would put together a book club, a baby shower, a birthday dinner, or even a Super Bowl party. Center the gathering around an activity like a meal or tea or wine. Even if you feel like you don't know enough people who would be interested, or you are new to an area, use social media to start a group. Create a Facebook or Eventbrite invite. If you just put the idea "out there," you may be surprised by how many people this resonates with. Write up a mission statement that briefly describes why you want to form this community. I always find it so interesting that the people in our circles who seem least likely to show up and participate in such a community are usually the ones who show up first.

Over time, as our group of women gathered again, we brainstormed self-care ideas, set self-care goals, and signed up for self-care activities together. We were always checking in with one another to find out how each person's self-care practice was going, what they needed to feel supported, and what obstacles others could remove to help them continue on their path. In a stern yet loving manner, we held one another accountable to do what we said we were going to do. For me, this was key because one of the things I hate the most is letting people down. Thus, in order to not disappoint my community of care, I would take care of myself.

Reflecting back, this seems almost comical. At that time, the main reason I didn't give up on myself was in order to not disappoint other people. In many ways, I felt obliged to do what I said I was going to do because I didn't want my character questioned and because I didn't want to let down the women who were showing up for me by not showing up for myself.

To be clear, while I was receiving support, I was also an ally for self-care to my friends. Self-care and community care aren't mutually exclusive. Uplifting the group wasn't any individual's responsibility, nor was practicing self-care solely on one's own shoulders. What I learned was that, when groups are dedicated to inner work, they create a collective energy that expands outward and augments each person's individual contribution to the collective rising.

This is not out of reach for anyone. A community of care doesn't start with two or more people — it starts within an individual who desires such a community. That person has done enough inner work to understand that they have work to do, and they gather a community of others who similarly recognize their own needs and are ready to work together. No one ever arrives at a community of care whole; everyone arrives fractured, bruised, and sometimes even skeptical. The only important thing is that everyone arrives.

Everyone's self-care journey will be different. I started mine by developing my own coping plan. As I saw clearly the obstacles and challenges in my path, I realized that some of my challenges were insurmountable on my own. So I gathered my friends and acquaintances for a fun evening of unwinding, and then I did one of the hardest things I've ever done: I asked for help. Once our community of care was established, each person created their own self-care plan, and we shared our plans with one another, including our obstacles and areas of need. We created a group structure by establishing monthly meetings and organizing those meetings to ensure that everyone had a chance to check in, ask for what they needed, and give what they could. Ultimately, this mutually beneficial web of women caring for one another was not only beautiful, it was life-saving and life-affirming.

CHAPTER EIGHT

Showing Up

The worst thing that happens in life is not death.
The worst thing would be to miss it....I think the
great danger in life is not showing up.

— RACHEL NAOMI REMEN

As a young girl up until I graduated high school, I used to spend my summers in Jerusalem, to visit family and deepen the connection with my culture. I always loved my time there, especially when I was a young adolescent, because I had more freedom and independence than I did back home. I could walk into the center of town and to the market; I could take the bus lines to visit cousins, to museums, and to the community pool. One summer, in the 1990s, my cousin and I stayed out later than usual, missing the final bus home. We decided to flag down a taxi; the cab driver who stopped for us rolled down his car window and asked, "Where to?" in Hebrew with an Arabic accent. I immediately responded — not thinking anything of it — with the name of the neighborhood, "Katamon."

My cousin whispered to me in Hebrew, "No, we can't get in. He is Palestinian." She waved him on.

I was troubled. "What do you mean?" I asked. "So what?"

"You don't understand," she snapped back. "You're American now. People like him, they want to kill us."

"What are you saying?! That's crazy!" I angrily replied.

For the next few days, I polled several of my aunts and uncles, cousins, anyone who would talk to me: "Is this true? Do all Palestinians want us dead?" Some answered, "Yes, of course, they killed your cousin so-and-so in 1948," or in 1967, 1973, or 1982. Others said, "Well, not all of them; some are good, but many aren't." Even as an adolescent, I could not accept this absurdity, this blanket truth. Weeks later, I was walking through the *souk* — a traditional open-air market — in the Old City, meandering through the Jewish Quarter, and I lost my way by making a wrong turn into the Muslim Quarter. All of the narratives I had heard played out in my head, and I was sure that I was never going to be seen again. "This time, when I am kidnapped," I told myself, "my parents will never find me." I stopped in my tracks, trying to remember any landmarks to help me navigate back to perceived safety.

I clearly looked incredibly frightened and lost because just then I felt a gentle tap on my shoulder. It was a boy, around my age — he spoke to me in Hebrew with a thick accent, the same accent as the taxi driver. "Are you lost?" I froze. The voices in my head were telling me to run, but my intuition and my heart were telling me to stay. This boy, who introduced himself as Ahmed, had shown up and was offering me his help.

I finally nodded. Ahmed took me by the arm and walked me

through the narrow corridors of the market, up and down stone steps, all the while telling me not to worry, that he would make sure I was safe. He led me back to the Jewish Quarter, where everything looked familiar to me again. I was so thrilled that I offered to buy him a popsicle on that warm summer day — he agreed. We sat together on the edge of a planter learning more about each other — our hobbies, favorite sports, music, dreams for the future. I recall Ahmed looking up at the sky dreamily and saying he wanted to visit America one day and then to travel the world. When I told him I was from Florida, he immediately asked if I was near Disney World.

In hindsight, I made the right turn that day. While I never saw Ahmed again, he planted a seed within me. I didn't make sense of it until years later, but I knew this: The boy I shared a popsicle with was just like me. He wanted to live a *big* life and make a difference in the world. We shared a common humanity. He showed up for me — without questioning my difference — and changed the dominant narrative and beliefs that I had about "people like him." This is the seed that Ahmed planted, one that bloomed many years later when I found myself in a living room drinking tea in a Palestinian village with a mother named Fatima.

Showing Up Doesn't Always Need to Be on Purpose

My friend Soren Gordhamer, the founder of Wisdom 2.0, an annual conference that explores the intersection of modern life and technology, once told me a story about how he used to take his young son to the local water park every summer. Each time, his son glanced up at the tallest waterslide, with its spiraling staircase, and remarked enthusiastically: "Next year, I'll be tall enough to go up there!" Finally, after several summers, his son reached the height requirement to climb those stairs and fulfill his dream of sliding down the "big boy" slide. As Soren watched his son's bobbing head, barely visible over the banister, make the ascent to the top landing, Soren rushed over to the pool where the slide spit out riders. As he waited earnestly for his son, he watched one exhilarated rider after another appear. After fifteen minutes, he felt a tap on the back of his arm. He spun around to find his son standing there looking distraught.

"What's up buddy? What happened? Is everything okay?"

"I was too scared to go down," his son explained. His son said he had stood watching person after person grab the overhang bar, sit down, and scoot forward, and he had attempted many times to do the same, but each time he hopped out of the wading pool and back onto the concrete. Finally, he resolved to walk down the stairs, head hanging low in disappointment. Soren said something to the effect of "We'll get 'em next time." The summer was long, and there would be plenty of opportunities to conquer the slide on their next visit to the park, but to his surprise, his son insisted on trying again right away. Soren chuckled and found inspiration in his son's resolve to tackle his fears head on and with such determination. He watched his son turn toward the stairs again and make his way back up. When he could no longer see him, he turned his attention to the pool, and again, person after person plunged off the slide's end, but not his son. After about ten minutes, Soren instinctively looked toward the stairs, and sure enough, a familiar blond-haired head was bobbing down and making its way toward him.

This routine happened several times in succession. Up and down, up and down … until finally, Soren saw his son's blond head coming down the slide, slowly winding its way around and back, until he eventually emerged in the pool. With incredible excitement, Soren entered the pool as his son swam over to him. His son had the widest smile, grinning from ear to ear and beaming with pride! Soren felt sympathetic joy and pride in his son. What a huge moment! As they exited the pool, Soren turned to his son and said, "Hey buddy, that was amazing! I am so impressed with your tenacity and resolve. I'm curious to know... what changed for you this last time? How did you finally get the courage to just go for it?"

His son stopped short, looked up at him with his big eyes, and said, "Well, Dad, I stood there holding the bar, and I got scared again, and I was about to come back down, and then... I just slipped!"

I love this story so much. It reminds me that we don't always have to be deliberately courageous in order to take the leap. We can accidentally slip into things that can be important, exhilarating, paradigm-shifting, and impactful. The most important thing we can do is just show up, intentionally and consistently. If we show up again and again, the chances of us taking the plunge in life's biggest moments — even if we are not entirely prepared — is almost guaranteed.

Show Up for Yourself First

The nine years between the first gathering of my formal community of care and the exact moment I started to truly show up for myself each and every day both intentionally and consistently — in November 2015 — are a blur. As I reflect back through the haze, I mostly recognize incremental progress that led me to that moment. About a year after the first community-of-care gathering, I was well on my way to stabilizing my eyesight and controlling the flare-ups, and I started showing up for myself in a big way. I was making progress as I settled into a routine with work, family, and friends. Life wasn't always easy, but I felt like I was getting the hang of things. Each day had its ups and downs, lifts and falls, but I was learning to ride the waves. My heart felt mended enough to think about dating again, and I put myself out there, but very slowly and on my own terms. What I refused to do was allow my friends to set me up on blind dates with someone they considered the "perfect person" for me. I wasn't the perfect person for myself yet, and so I knew better than to jump into the dating scene — with a young child in tow — without fully understanding what I wanted out of myself, this life, and a partner.

It was not anyone else's job to design my path for me. I had to create my own future and manifest my own destiny. *Destiny is choice, not chance.* I knew I had to choose to show up for myself first — even if sometimes accidentally — before I could expect anyone to show up for me, and before I could consistently show up for others. Showing up for ourselves requires a number of things — faith, trust, wisdom, courage. It also requires the willingness to crawl into a "black box."

I didn't encounter the concept of a black box until 2014, when I was listening to the "Black Box" episode of *Radiolab* on NPR. I almost didn't listen to the segment, thinking the show was about the airplane recording device. I became intrigued when the show defined this black box as "those peculiar spaces where it's clear what's going in, we know what's coming out, but what happens in between is a mystery." The first example was something that is incredibly familiar — how a caterpillar becomes a butterfly. Almost everyone learns about this process in preschool: The caterpillar builds a cocoon around itself, and when it comes out again, it's transformed into a butterfly. But what happens inside the chrysalis during this gestation period? My preschool lessons were vague about this, and I'd always imagined a step-by-step process: The caterpillar changed, growing new limbs and wings, until it had a new body. But no, this is wrong.

As *Radiolab* informed me, if one were to open a chrysalis after a week, all one would find inside is "goo" or slime. There would be no discernible caterpillar or anything, only a formless, gelatinous substance. In order for a caterpillar to become a butterfly, a caterpillar digests itself through the release of enzymes that break down its body. This "goo" is a collection of what are aptly called *imaginal cells*. Not unlike stem cells, these imaginal cells contain the instructions to create the butterfly, and eventually, the goo reforms into wings, legs, antennae — until the butterfly is complete.

Obviously, the caterpillar doesn't decide to one day become a butterfly. This "desire" is encoded into its DNA. The caterpillar probably has no idea what will happen within the cocoon it spins. However, in my — perhaps romantic — estimation, the caterpillar knows one thing. It has to show up. It has to build, trusting in whatever comes next. It must have self-confidence, feel worthy, be fearless! It gorges for days and days, plumping itself up in preparation for … its own destruction.

That evening, sitting at home after another failed date, my wormy self realized that for a long time I had been stewing in a black box. We, too, have imaginal cells, and if we take a leap of faith and allow ourselves to stew in them, if we are brave enough to step outside of what we know (whether what we know is comfortable or uncomfortable), we might find ourselves transforming. I reflected back on the courage I had to show up for my son and start a new life for him (and for us) after illness and divorce. I was committed to my own evolution and to building structures of support around me. But I still did not fully believe in my ability to imagine a different future for myself, one that was not dictated by social norms, by familial or cultural expectations. I did not trust myself to make decisions of the heart, to know what was "good for me." I trusted the opinions of others far more than my own. I was not showing up for myself. But I was, I realized, in the active process of self-obliteration. I was in a black box — so to speak — without knowing what I wanted to become, or how I might emerge, because I was too busy being the sort of caterpillar I thought the world wanted or expected me to be.

Caterpillars have a lot to teach us about how we can navigate through the transitions of life. I spent a greater part of my life believing that transitions only have two real stages: before change and after change. Before college, after college. Before marriage, after marriage. Before parenthood, after parenthood. The first stage is a time of preparation. We soak in and feed ourselves with the knowledge, experiences, and tools necessary to get to the next stage. The second stage, "after change," is when we become what we've been preparing for — a butterfly. We often expect that transition to happen quickly, or better yet immediately, and with little further effort or pain. The caterpillar reminds us that there is a middle or third stage — the ambiguous black box.

In the transitory black box stage, we are neither who we were before nor what we will be after. We are formless "goo," and that makes us fearful of the outcome. What if we lose ourselves or, even worse, morph into something or someone we don't want or don't like? We forget that what we become is forged from who we are and who we were. Our imaginal cells — the essence of our being — are still "us." Changes are meant to be gooey; they are meant to be ambiguous. Yet even though the person we are doesn't remain intact, we do not completely disappear. Our only job is to show up for ourselves with complete faith — in the process, in our evolution, in ourselves. Then when we emerge, when we exit the black box of our cocoon in all of our newfound glory, we are able to do two things: We attract other "butterflies" into our space, and we have the capacity to fully show up for others.

As I emerged from the black box of all my "after" stages — after my divorce, after my grief, after my self-flagellation, after questioning my self-worth, after my understanding that I have what it takes to battle my chronic eye disease — interesting things began to unfold. I met my now-husband, Jason, I found a job that was fulfilling, and I shifted from always leaning on my community of care to mostly supporting them. I deliberately use the term *unfold* because the process took a long time and many steps, and the after of something is always still the before to something else.

See You on the Sand

A year or so later, by late October 2015, life was going well, at least on paper. I was in a happy marriage to a wonderful man, I had a healthy son who was doing well in school, and I was doing better financially and professionally than I ever had before. While I was still dealing with my ongoing eye issues, I was managing to keep severe vision loss at bay. Still, even though I was showing up for work, for my son and husband, for my family, and for my community-at-large, I was not showing up for myself as often as I needed or wanted to. Due to my work travel schedule, I wasn't as plugged into my community of care as I had been, and I was craving connection. I remembered those evenings as a single mom, when Liam was in bed or at his father's house, when I had time for long meditation sits, for deep journaling, and for intense thinking. The hectic stressors of everyday life weren't allowing for that, and I longed for that feeling of connection that I once felt to myself and to the women in my community of care.

And so, in a spontaneous moment, I found myself staring at my Facebook page and decided to post the following message on my wall:

"If I taught meditation on a Sunday morning, who would join me? And where would we meet up?"

To my surprise, within an hour I had more than twenty responses from friends and acquaintances, ranging from "I'm in!" to "I really need this in my life right now." After a few days of going back and forth and investigating potential convenient locations, I settled on Hollywood North Beach Park in Hollywood, Florida, a public-access beach with plenty of parking and no obstructions from condominiums — a rarity in South Florida — on Sunday, November 15, at 8:30 in the morning. I created a Facebook invite with all the details and sent it to those who had indicated interest. I gave the event a title: "Cease & Exist." On the Saturday evening before our gathering, I checked the weather report, which called for high winds with gusts of up to twenty-five miles per hour — not hospitable for beachgoers and certainly not conducive for meditation. "You're still going?" my husband, Jason, asked.

"Of course," I responded. He rolled his eyes and knew that it was useless to argue with me. Secretly, I hoped that the meteorologists' predictions would change overnight, as they sometimes do, and that I would wake up to a sunny morning. But alas, nature had other plans. At 6 a.m., I opened the back door to let the dogs out into the backyard before I left, and I witnessed the chop of the pool water and the fronds of the palm trees violently swaying to and fro, bending to the point that I thought they were going to snap. "Show up," I muttered to myself. "You are going to show up."

I gathered my beach towels and grabbed a hoody, added some fresh coffee to my mug, and headed for the front door. Jason walked into the living room and harkened, "Hey! You're still going!? It's crazy out there. No one is going to show up."

I responded: "I am going to show up."

For thirty minutes, I drove in silence all the way to the beach. When I pulled up to the parking lot in front of the beach, the booth attendant looked surprised to see a car. I rolled down my window to pay, and she waived me in, probably thinking that I would not manage to stay put for more than a few minutes. I parked and scoped out the spot where we were supposed to meditate. The dark, ominous sky was threatening to unleash a serious amount of rain, each cloud like a saturated sponge about to be squeezed. The boardwalk was mostly covered in blown sand, and as I reached the short wooden pathway leading to the beach, I had to fight to keep my eyes open in the fierce winds. My hair was tousled, and pinpricks of sand painfully abraded my face.

I walked back toward the car and checked the time on my phone. It was seven minutes past eight. I decided to wait until quarter after to see if anybody else showed up. Rather than sit in my car, I resolved to sit in a crabgrass patch near the concrete path, a spot partially shielded from the wind by the sea grape trees and my car. I rolled out my towel and sat cross-legged, closing my eyes and placing my palms on my heart. *If I can meditate here*, I thought, *I can meditate anywhere*. After a few minutes, I opened my eyes, and to my delight, I saw two women in the distance approaching me with their rolled-up towels. My heart jumped. I felt so validated to have shown up, and I am certain they were relieved to see me. They sat down in front of me, and soon more friends joined, one at a time, until by quarter to nine, twelve of us were sitting in basically a patch of dirt in the parking lot, sheltered by sea grapes. We formed a small circle and faced one another. I paused to smile and gaze upon everyone's face as we fully arrived in the moment. Then I gave a lesson about meditation, went through a few breathing exercises, and asked everyone to close their eyes. Small ants were crawling on my towel and up my leg, but that was irrelevant. All that mattered to me in that moment was that I was leading my first guided meditation.

We meditated in these inhospitable conditions for twenty-five straight minutes, and when it was over, the wind seemed to momentarily stop. There was calm, a silence before the storm. For a few minutes, we shared our experiences, and then we felt the first drops of rain begin to fall. A torrential Florida downpour was moments away, and we hustled to gather our belongings and get in our cars. As we exchanged brief hugs, my friend Jessica asked, "Will we meet again soon?"

"Of course!" I responded without hesitation. As I crawled into the front seat of my car, the sky broke open, and I sat and listened to the drops as they pelted the roof of my car. I exhaled and smiled, giving myself a little nod of credit for the small success that day. I planted a seed. I started a ripple. I felt something shift — I didn't then know what — but I knew I would keep going with this flow to find out.

When I got home I modified the Facebook event and changed the date to two weeks from Sunday. I posted the link on my wall with a short message about the morning's experience. Fourteen days later, on a sunny day, when I returned to the same beach, twenty people showed up. And the following week, thirty people showed up, not all of whom I knew. Each Sunday gathering brought out new friends, old friends, passersby who were curious about our gathering, and friends of friends who saw a post shared on Facebook. In late January 2016, as the gathering was nearing seventy people, I came home and announced to Jason that I needed to purchase a small portable microphone and speaker.

"Why?" he asked.

"Because the people in the back can't always hear me above the waves crashing ashore." He seemed perplexed by the phrase "people in the back."

"Who are these people?"

"I don't know all of them, but this is starting to gain momentum, and we are starting to build a community. There is something magical happening. There was a *before*, and now I feel like I am in a black box, but I don't know how I am going to emerge yet." Now he was even more confused. Still, he went online that afternoon and helped me order a portable speaker and microphone. A month later, I returned home to announce that I needed a wireless PA system that could amplify my voice even more.

"Why?" he asked, surprised.

"Because I have close to two hundred people each week now. And they can't hear me with this little microphone when they are all spread out."

"What!? That's incredible! Are you serious?"

"Yes, I am totally serious. I struck some sort of chord with people. I don't know why they keep showing up and multiplying. We all need each other...." I trailed off.

That afternoon, we bought a large rechargeable, portable

speaker with a tripod stand, and the following weekend, Jason came down to the beach to "help me" work the speaker. Really, I think he wanted to bear witness and get a better understanding of what was happening. The speaker had Bluetooth capabilities, and so I decided to curate a playlist of my favorite songs about peace and happiness. As soon as I got to the beach, before anybody showed up, I connected my speaker to my phone and hit play. Familiar guitar chords and a harmonica belted out, then the distinct voice of Bob Dylan. Others in my ever-growing playlist were Pink Floyd, Coldplay, Marvin Gaye, and the Pixies. The music greeted the hundreds of people gathering each week, until eventually we expanded with additional speakers, daisy-chaining them together, twenty feet or so apart. By Mother's Day weekend in May 2016, almost six months to the day after I had showed up for the first time, we had over one thousand people gathering to meditate, filling up every inch of the beach from the dunes to the shoreline.

I often asked myself why people were attracted to the gathering — I couldn't believe for one second or give myself credit that it had anything to do with me. I was just the conduit, I told myself; I was the pebble thrower. But now and again I got a handwritten note or a direct message into my social media inbox, or someone stayed after class to give me a hug and cry on my shoulder. They told me things like: I feel welcome; it is the first time I felt unintimidated when trying to meditate; I appreciate your honesty about your struggles in the talk before the guided meditation; thank you for being real and relatable; thank you for making this free and open to everyone. Reflecting back, I am most proud of the community we built, which has managed to sustain itself ever since that fateful day I chose to sit in a windstorm rather than sleep in. For over five years and counting, our "sand tribe" has managed to ensure that there are no barriers to entry — not finances, not stigmas, not age or gender, religious affiliation, or level of experience. We remain open and free to all. The music is familiar, the location is naturally relaxing, and our sacred space is a place where an old Jewish woman from Brooklyn can sit next to a Black lesbian from the Caribbean, who is next to a tatted-up biker dude with a mohawk and a leather vest. It's a weekly drug-free Burning Man gathering on a beach instead of in the middle of a desert, full of love and acceptance.

The Power of Five

Through the spring of 2016, each weekend I led guided meditations on the beach, holding a space for all who showed up and feeling increasingly fulfilled, inspired, and moved to tears from sympathetic joy and sadness. In those moments, for the few hours I was on that cushion, holding the microphone in my hand and observing people slow down and deliberately pause to tend to themselves, I felt aligned with my purpose. Then, on Monday morning, I would return to my "real job" in the corporate world, feeling emptier and emptier.

However, I continued to show up for my corporate role as the head of a midsize firm with over two thousand employees, while also showing up each Sunday to support a growing community of thousands of meditators, but the two loads were too heavy. I couldn't keep holding on to both. My heart was telling me which path to take — the one where I knew I would show up for myself, as a fully emerged butterfly — but my head was keeping me from taking the leap and trusting in my abilities. In terms of my work, a lot of people depended on me. My income was important for our family, and the company I helmed provided a livelihood for its employees. Yet with each passing Monday morning ride into work, the knot in my stomach grew larger and the feeling of emptiness and dissatisfaction stirred in me like a tiger pacing in a cage, ready to pounce. Something had to give.

At times, we have to let go of what is to make room for what will be. That is another meaning of the black box. Of course, the very idea of change — small or major — usually produces at least some discomfort and agita. When I finally took a leap of faith and resigned from my well-paying job to become a full-time meditation teacher, most people thought I had lost my mind. The final straw that broke the camel's back and pushed me to hand in my resignation notice in July 2016 was a comment that my then-fourteen-year-old son, Liam, said to me when I came home from work after a long day and an even longer commute. He was sitting at the kitchen table, eating dinner with his pajamas on, and I was practically in tears and not interested in talking about anyone's day but my own because I just wanted to vent about my misery.

Liam looked me square in the eyes and confidently proclaimed, "You know what would be the best day of my life?"

"What?" I asked, expecting he would say finally leaving our house and my madness behind.

"When you finally quit that damn job and take your own advice!"

Ouch. That one stung. That evening, I wrote my letter of resignation. I dated it for two months from that day. I knew I needed to have a definitive date, but I also wanted some time to work through every aspect of this decision and have some semblance of a plan before I took this leap of faith.

Intellect and logic are certainly useful tools for working through certain issues, but it is also easy to overthink and become paralyzed by analysis. I think the truth is that, when making decisions that require placing a bet on ourselves, the real question we are always trying to answer is: How can I be sure I will succeed? When faced with these types of decisions, we are sharply aware of every door we might close, while being unable to see all the doors that might open. Hindsight is a beautiful thing. The trouble is that it shadows our foresight.

The term "leap of faith" is a fitting metaphor. There is no answer to the question, How can I be sure I will succeed? There are no guarantees in life. Yet despite this uncertainty, we choose to take leaps of faith, and with this choice, we boldly declare to the universe: I trust in me and ... I trust in you.

In my increasing misery and discomfort, the universe sent me a sign from a fourteen-year-old boy, wiser than his years on this planet. He was watching me, a scorekeeper for the universe. He knew how to verbalize that something had to give. He saw I had become like a proverbial frog in a boiling pot of my own making, and he knew it would take an Indiana Jones–size boulder rolling toward me to finally get me to move. Something interesting happened after I wrote that resignation letter, similar to what happened when I started to journal after my divorce — taking this leap of faith became real and attainable, and somehow, it didn't seem absurd.

On a Friday morning exactly one month before my intended resignation date, I changed the date on the top of my letter, hit print, and signed the bottom. Feeling anxious, I walked down the corridor to the office of the owner of the company, sat down in the chair across from his desk, and handed him the letter to read in front of me. While I did feel a sense of relief that this formality was over and that I no longer had to live with this secret burden, the sense of euphoria I thought I would feel never came. Instead, what entered me was fear. After the deed was done, I found myself asking, *What the heck did I just do?*

I find it interesting that people tend to skip over these moments when they share their own stories about leaps of faith. Maybe they don't want to admit to fear, or maybe in hindsight, after things work out and time passes, they forget how scary it first was. What keeps most of us standing at the edge afraid to take the leap is fear that things won't work out, and right after taking a leap, fear can make us think we have made a huge mistake. It seems like we are in free fall, and so we desperately try to figure out a way to get back to the ledge. This is understandable and maybe even expected. When we make a huge life change that requires leaving behind our comfort zone, we can feel vulnerable, exposed, and inadequate. We are no longer a caterpillar, but for the moment, we aren't yet a butterfly, either. However, *the absence of euphoric excitement is not an indicator that you have made the wrong decision.*

When I found myself struggling with self-doubt and worry after my resignation, I sought to calm and focus myself using an exercise called the "Power of Five." In essence, this asks you to imagine what your life would look like if you did or did not go ahead with a decision. Specifically, I asked myself: If I went ahead with my decision, what would my life look like in five weeks? In five months? In five years? Then I asked the inverse: If I didn't resign and take this leap, what would my life look like in five weeks, five months, and five years?

Such a simple tool, but incredibly powerful. Changing what no longer works for us, whatever it might be, is so brave. To be able to stand up and declare that "this no longer works for me" is a declaration of self-love and self-worth and an acknowledgment that we are capable of doing more and being more. It is how we show up for ourselves first. Only then can we do more and be of service to the world.

How Showing Up for Ourselves Helps Others

It bears repeating: We cannot truly show up for others if we do not show up for ourselves first. There is an undeniable and intricate connection between our inner work and the outer world.

But also, just as importantly, our personal example of showing up for ourselves can ignite and inspire others to do the same in their own lives. And part of showing up means taking the risk to be part of others' lives. Just being present for someone is a deeply divine act, something that I believe is the ultimate gift we were made to share with others.

Like making life changes, this happens in ways big and small. I am a big fan of incremental change, of "eating the elephant one bite at a time." Showing up for ourselves can be as simple as arriving on time — or waking up on time. It might mean effective communication when plans change, things come up, and life happens. It might mean standing up for ourselves with the sole purpose of being understood, not validated. This is sometimes described as being in "integrity with oneself." If we are clear on our values and intentions, we can keep ourselves more balanced despite what is going on around us.

Those in our immediate community — friends, family, co-workers, and others whose lives intersect with ours — see what we do, and this alone can directly affect them. But more importantly, how we show up for and take care of ourselves affects our ability to show up for others. This includes how we have worked through our intergenerational trauma and "the way we grew up." This can affect our interactions, our ability to collaborate and compromise, what our "nonnegotiables" are, and how we hold ourselves and others accountable.

We have been affected by others and external circumstances since the day we were born, and these things influence the goals we have for ourselves and how we relate to the people in our life. For example, as a child, when we broke a rule or went back on an agreement, what were the ramifications? If this involved hurtful or unhealthy behaviors that still influence us as adults, then we risk repeating these harmful patterns with others. If we aren't capable of taking care of our personal needs first, this can affect the kinds of relationships we create and the types of commitments we make. If we struggle to connect with others in healthy ways, it will be difficult to show up in support of them in the ways they need. For instance, if we haven't worked through our own stuff, we are more likely as adults to project those unresolved issues onto others. In other words, we might think we are showing up, but we aren't actually open to what another person is going through. To show up for someone else means, as much as possible, coming from a curious, seeking-to-understand place. This can be really difficult to do if most of our emotional and physical energy is focused on our own needs and problems. To some extent, we always have personal issues to deal with — life is always happening — so when showing up for others, always check in with yourself first, figure out what is or is not within your ability to do, adjust what you want to commit to, decide if you must let something go, and as needed, verbalize and explain what is going on for you and what you see going on with the other person. Being honest about our limits is also part of showing up.

Something interesting happens when we do all of this "showing up," tending first to ourselves and *then* directly showing up for immediate community members: We heal ourselves, which in turn helps to heal others, whose lives we touch and impact, which in turn empowers them to do the same for others. This helps us build and reinforce those true communal safety nets that set the stage for cultural and societal shifts, for movements to occur.

The call to action is this: How can you hold yourself accountable to show up as the best version of yourself in as many moments as possible? Can you be fully present to the presence of others, thereby strengthening your relationship with them? Can you draw a correlation between your interaction with others and their future interaction with the people they come into contact with? The choice is ours in each and every moment, but deciding becomes easier when our values are clear.

CHAPTER NINE

Circles of Influence and the Ripple Effect

Example is not the main thing in influencing others.
It is the only thing.

— ALBERT SCHWEITZER

Through the summer, as the meditation community grew bigger Sunday after Sunday, society itself was gearing up for the 2016 US presidential election. I was determined to be apolitical, so that everyone would feel welcome, but that promise didn't last long. In the early morning of Sunday, June 12, at 2 a.m., a gunman opened fire at the Pulse nightclub in Orlando, killing forty-nine people and wounding fifty-three. When I heard the news that morning, no one yet knew exactly how many people were dead or injured, but the atrocity of the mass shooting was too much to bear. I knew that I needed to offer some healing words for the people who would arrive at the beach to meditate that morning, and I sat down to write some talking points. As I did, my anger grew over the failure of our lawmakers to make significant changes to gun laws after Columbine, Aurora, and Sandy Hook. I didn't know all the details about this shooting, but I knew for sure that somewhere along the line, there had been a failure to address the mental health of the shooter, and if it had been addressed, this tragedy might have been prevented.

Among the people at the beach meditation that morning were several individuals who knew people killed in the shooting; they came to our gathering looking for peace, solace, and solidarity. Others hadn't heard anything, and upon arrival, as they unfolded their towels, they were told the shocking news, which spread quietly like a wildfire of whispers. I made a decision that morning — partly from a place of rage, but I'd like to believe mostly from wanting to mend the torn fabric of the world — to speak up about gun violence, specific types of gun ownership, background checks, and other gun measures that need to be in place, in addition to the mental health crisis in the United States. I knew some people sitting in our community would not agree with my viewpoints; some might even find them abhorrent. I felt a responsibility to speak out anyway. After the session ended that morning, a few people came up to me to express their disappointment that I was speaking about political topics, though it was a topic that, oddly enough, I did not even think should be controversial. But most of the people, whether in person or via messages, both in the moment and days after, told me how much they appreciated what I said.

As summer turned to fall and the presidential election neared between Donald Trump and Hillary Clinton, I faced a similar quandary. Each week some attendees showed up wearing a shirt or a hat in support of their candidate, and I reiterated the message that we needed to be tolerant of one another; we needed to be open, to have mindful conversations, and to remain hopeful that, as Martin Luther King Jr. said, "the arc of the moral universe is long, but it bends toward justice." The million-dollar question was: If I shared my unfiltered opinions, would people still feel welcome? Should I speak up about the candidate I would vote for? Should I canvas for local candidates and amendments I support? Or should I remain a bipartisan, noncontroversial meditation teacher who turns away from political involvement? Ideally, I wanted to have the opportunity to express my opinions and still welcome the people who didn't share my views.

The quest to find the answer led me to dive deeper into the examination of my responsibility as a community organizer, a teacher, and (gasp!) an influencer. I was beginning to understand the responsibility of having a platform and the power of having an influence on others. To be clear, I believe *we all* have a platform and *we all* have influence. You don't need to be an "influencer" as defined by today's social media. Further, influence can also be negative, promoting selfishness, manipulation, and immorality. But influence as a concept is neither good nor bad. It is a neutral force that can be used for any pursuit. We exercise influence to persuade and gain consent, whether consciously or not.

In his widely respected book, *Pre-Suasion: A Revolutionary Way to Influence and Persuade*, author Robert Cialdini identified through his research that the more we perceive people to be part of "us" — meaning in the same group, community, or category of people — the more likely we'll be influenced by them. He calls this the "unity" principle. "It's about the categories that individuals use to define themselves and their groups, such as race, ethnicity, nationality, and family, as well as political and religious affiliations," Cialdini writes. "A key characteristic of these categories is that their members tend to feel at one with, merged with, the others. They are the categories in which the conduct of one member influences the self-esteem of other members. Simply put, we is the shared me." In its simplest form, the unity principle can be boiled down to the third principle in Maslow's hierarchy of needs (see figure), which is the human need to belong.

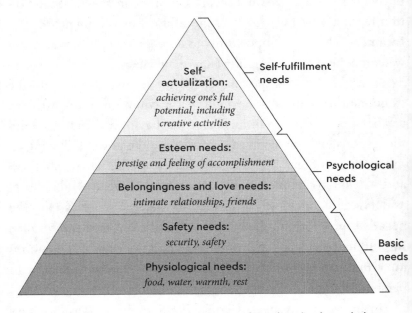

Source: Saul McLeod, "Maslow's Hierarchy of Needs," SimplyPsychology, December 29, 2020, https:simplypsychology.org/maslow.

Why is this important? Because when humans feel like they belong to a group, they are more likely to be open to persuasion. But with influence comes great responsibility. In my newfound role, I had a proverbial soapbox on the sand, and I knew people were listening to my opinions and watching my actions intently. I also knew that, based on the unity principle, I had a unique opportunity to make every attendee of our weekly gatherings feel a bond with everyone else and feel like they were part of a collective group and experience. The kind of thing that, if they happened to see someone at a coffee shop or supermarket, they would feel an immediate bond or kinship: "Ah! You attend meditation on the beach on Sundays. So do I!"

Cialdini writes about how unity can be created by sharing an experience or through cocreation. The sand tribe gatherings, as we began to call them, managed to do both: They offered a shared experience that was only available because people showed up, week after week, contributing to the cocreation of the space. When creating a community of care, it is important to remember this unity principle, which is all about appealing to *we* — a cohesive identity that is shared by the group. In my humble opinion, cocreation is one of the most impactful and sustainable ways to bring diverse people together, to get them to create a bond, and to influence them to speak and listen to one another. The most basic bond of all is our common humanity. When applied judiciously and authentically, I have found that, like the effects of a pebble thrown into a pond, the ripples of unity continue to radiate.

Drop a Pebble, Start a Ripple

The Dalai Lama once said, "Just as ripples spread out when a single pebble is dropped into water, the actions of individuals can have far-reaching effects." After showing up, remember that having an impact does not require a grand gesture. Even small actions can have a positive impact. The only thing required is momentum, built on consistent, small actions that shift the status quo. Sometimes, you may see and feel the results of the ripple right away;

sometimes the ripple effect may not be felt for weeks, months, or longer; sometimes you may never know the effect of your actions. Drop the pebble, anyway.

Think about the big bang — yes, *the* big bang. Consider the universe, which was created from a single burst of energy — planets, galaxies, life in exponential forms, and the creation of *you*. It all started with one, singular event. A ripple in the fabric of space, something that emanated from seemingly nothing. We each have this piece of "godliness" in us — we are each divine creators in our own right. We can create something out of nothing, and perhaps even more importantly, we can continue to cocreate as our actions ripple out. Rest assured, the ripples will continue to spread far and wide, but if you choose to deliberately ride or follow them, they will lead you to places beyond your imagination.

Perhaps this sounds far too simplistic to work. Perhaps, if we were standing face to face, you would squint your eyes at me and say, "Shelly, are you for real? Are you telling me to chunk problems out into small pieces and then just show up? That's it?" I would look you square in the eyes and reply yes, without even so much as blinking. Unequivocally, yes.

In early March 2020, at the beginning of the Covid-19 pandemic, I was sitting at my kitchen table scrolling through messages and reading emails about the closures that were starting to happen across the country and that inevitably would soon happen in Florida, too. Half the messages were fearful and panicked — about how sheltering at home would mean no work, no work would mean no income, and no income would mean no groceries, gas, phone, or electricity. Other messages were from people in my community asking me what they could do to help others in need, since traditional volunteering opportunities were not going to be possible during quarantine. I knew that — using a mutual-aid model — connecting those in need directly with donors who could fulfill that need would be an efficient way to get help to people in a time of disconnection and anxiety.

I went online and created two simple Google forms: one entitled "Give Help" and the other "Get Help." I hoped that by posting them on my social media accounts with a brief explanation, I could amass a few dozen people in need of essential items and a few dozen people who could help. I would then connect the two parties directly via email or text message and step out of the way, allowing them to figure out how best to transact. I posted the links and went to bed, never fathoming that when I woke up the next day each form would be filled out by hundreds upon hundreds of individuals. As I scrolled through the names of the individuals on each spreadsheet, I realized that I only knew a handful of them; many had different area codes and even different country codes. The post went viral and kicked off what I eventually called Pandemic of Love — a global, grassroots, mutual-aid organization.

Within a few weeks, I replicated the forms for different communities across the globe and trained other people to form chapters. Within a few months, Pandemic of Love had hundreds of volunteers and chapters in over a dozen countries across the world. Within twelve months, the organization managed to match over 1.5 million people, and donors directly transacted over fifty-four million dollars to people in need with no overhead or administrative fees (for more on this, see page 167). Early on, when the organization was nearing ten thousand matches, I had a video conference call with my dear friend and mentor Scott Rogers, the director of the Mindfulness in Law Program and a lecturer in law at the University of Miami. After catching up and discussing the uncharted landscape of the pandemic, Scott asked me about Pandemic of Love.

"Well, I 'accidentally' started this movement — I replied, using my fingers to signal air quotes, when Scott raised his hand and interrupted.

"Uh-huh, no. Once is an accident. Twice is a coincidence. Three times is a pattern."

What Scott said was undeniably true and gave me pause. Showing up on a blustery beach day to teach meditation and starting a meditation community that grew into a movement, *that* could be deemed an accident. But so many other times I had simply "showed up" in a way that revealed an indisputable pattern: I would have an emotional reaction to an event or occurrence; I'd become self-aware of the reaction; I'd pause and ask, "What can I do about it?"; and then I'd make a conscious decision to respond by showing up fully, with an open heart, in whatever way felt appropriate.

Case in point: When Liam was ten years old, he had a joint birthday party with his friend Evan, and they both decided to give up all their presents and ask their friends to instead donate money to help fund a music program at an underserved elementary school. Liam and Evan both played instruments and wanted to make sure that other children had an opportunity to do the same. The birthday party raised an astounding seven thousand dollars in donations on behalf of the VH1 Save the Music Foundation. When I contacted the organization, they asked me to send them the check and promised to send a certificate of appreciation to Liam and Evan. I explained to the coordinator that we wouldn't turn the funds over unless the kids had an opportunity to go visit a school where their funds would be used to support a music program, so they could actually see where their efforts were going.

Save the Music connected us to Canal Point Elementary School in Pahokee, Florida. I had grown up in South Florida, and I had never heard of Pahokee, but like a dutiful mom, I put the school's address into my GPS and drove Liam, Evan, and his mom, Beth, to the school. Palm Beach County is one of the richest counties in the United States, so I was pretty shocked that it contained a school that needed this kind of support. But as we left the main highway and drove west toward Lake Okeechobee, I began to wonder if the address I had put into my phone was wrong. Pahokee is one of the poorest towns in the Sunshine State. Its residents face immense financial struggle, particularly since the closure of the main sugar factory, which eliminated hundreds of jobs. Driving through miles of sugar cane fields and past small shacks felt like entering the Deep South of a hundred years ago.

Once at Canal Point Elementary, we were greeted by the band teacher, Mr. Goindoo, or Mr. G as the students called him. Mr. G walked us to the band room, which on the surface looked like every other band room I had ever seen, but upon closer inspection, I saw that many of the instruments were incredibly old and broken. Mr. G was not only a music teacher but also an instrument repairman. As the bell rang, students filed in and took their seats, moved their music stands into position, and got their instruments ready. "Welcome to the Hope Symphony!" Mr. G enthusiastically proclaimed. He introduced Evan and Liam to the class and offered them each a band chair — Evan on guitar and Liam on drums. Then, with a wave of a hand and a "one, two, three," everyone played, and our children, who came from incredibly privileged circumstances, connected immediately with kids who experienced food insecurity, instability in their family life, exposure to gun violence, drug addiction, and a myriad of other travesties. That day we showed up for Pahokee, we presented them with an oversize check, we connected with the children … and we drove home in our SUV to our comfortable suburban homes to have dinner with our families.

I could not stop thinking about the children at Canal Point: the girl with the sneaker that had the front cut off so her toes could poke through; the boy with the ill-fitting school uniform at least two sizes too small; the girl who was hunched over because she was embarrassed not to have a bra. I reached out to Mr. G the next day to thank him for his hospitality and told him that I wanted to do more. I wanted to come back and bring people with me, to enlist donors and make sure all these children had shoes and uniforms and brand-new instruments. I left Pahokee that day, but Pahokee didn't leave me. I went to work and showed up again a month later with bags of uniforms and new shoes for every child in the band program; two months later I showed up with donors for the end-of-year concert and with refurbished laptops; and during the summer I ran a fundraiser to help pay for summer band camp. Over nine years later, I am still showing up — bringing more resources, new recruits, and more donations. Over the years, Mr. G and I have partnered to expand the Hope Symphony to the point where Mr. G has finally been officially recognized for his tireless efforts to help kids find a "way out" of Pahokee, other than with a football scholarship. To use Scott's words, helping to grow and nurture a thriving, award-winning organization that breeds successful, college-bound musicians from the poorest area in Florida has not been an accident.

Another example: In January 2017, I flew to Washington, DC, with three girlfriends to attend the Women's March — an inspiring day that energized us and gave us some hope after months of grief and fear of the unknown after the November 2016 election of President Donald Trump. After the march ended, my girlfriends and I headed to a restaurant, where we drank wine and recounted the day's events, enjoying with pride all the other women around us in their knitted pink pussy hats. But something gnawed at me and I blurted it out: "What do we do now? Now that the march is over, what do we do when we fly back home?" We all looked at one another, exhausted from being on our feet for over fifteen hours, and stared blankly. Nothing was resolved over dinner.

However, that night, as I watched news footage of the day's events, I picked up my phone and created a Facebook event called "South Florida Women Rise Up." I selected a date exactly four weeks away, to give us time to plan. I posted the link to the event on my personal page and went to bed. The next morning, I had over five hundred Facebook alerts, and by the afternoon, over eight hundred women had RSVP'd to the event — whose location was still listed as "TBD." My friends Ina, Miro, and Meredith went to work crafting an agenda and inviting guest speakers from the Florida Women's March organization, including local representatives from the state and from Congress. I called my friend Lisa, who owns a restaurant in Fort Lauderdale, and asked her if we could hold the meeting, not *in* the restaurant, but in the restaurant parking lot. She was taken aback but agreed. On the day of the inaugural South Florida Women Rise Up gathering, over 450 women, men, and children showed up with folding chairs and towels ready to mobilize. The group continued to meet monthly throughout the year, and then it organized online for over four years until the 2020 election. Once again, in Scott's words, this was not an accident.

A final example: In 2018, after the tragic mass shooting at Marjory Stoneman Douglas High School in Parkland, Florida, which resulted in the murder of seventeen innocent lives, my meditation teacher, Sharon Salzberg, asked me how she could show up for our community. The national March for Our Lives event was over, and yet suffering in the community continued (and still does to this day). She offered to come and hold a meditation retreat for anyone in the community who wanted to show up; I was incredibly excited by the prospect of this offering, and I went to work. My friend Samantha and I found a location, secured sponsors, and promoted the event, to be held six months after the date of the shooting. Ultimately, hundreds of community members showed up for a half-day retreat on a Sunday morning, including parents whose children were murdered and/or injured, teachers from the school, and fellow students, neighbors, and friends of the victims. After the retreat ended, the parent of a student who was a victim of the shooting stayed behind to thank Sharon, Samantha, and me for organizing the event. He then confessed that this was one of the only times since the shooting that he had been able to quiet his mind and find peace, and he asked how he could access more of that feeling. A teacher, standing behind him, joined in and said that she finally felt like she had "permission to heal."

Showing up for Parkland, not knowing if anyone would attend the event, wound up setting off a chain of subsequent gatherings and events that led to additional retreats for gun-violence survivors — not just from Parkland but from all over the country, in communities affected by mass shootings and those affected by gun violence every day. Sharon and I, and so many incredible volunteer teachers and therapists, were able to create a safe space for healing and build a community that provided tools to individuals dealing with trauma. Again, this was not an accident.

Pushing the Boundaries of Influence

As I reviewed these events, the pattern became obvious: When we consistently show up and enact incremental, small actions, this creates a ripple effect emanating from our circles of influence; many small ripples create waves of change. Oftentimes we tend to segregate "circles of influence" from "circles of concern," two terms that are usually portrayed as nested circles. The larger circle is our "circle of concern," which refers to what concerns us but which we can't directly influence or change (like the economy, climate change, and so on). Inside this is a smaller "circle of influence," which refers to what concerns us and which we can do something about. But I would argue, based on my own experience, that thinking we have no influence in our circle of concern is wrong. I think — no, *I know* — that we can continuously expand our circle of influence outward toward the edges of our circle of concern, and eventually, sometimes, we can superimpose them, one on top of the other. Our circles of influence, like the ripples in a pond, can be ever-expanding, like the universe, if we keep showing up and committing incremental acts of kindness, which cause an impactful experience or which change an event's trajectory or somebody's mind.

Since I am at the center of my own circle of influence, I often start with a simple question: What can I do? I then expand out to consider my immediate community and those whom I can easily access and influence, asking: What can we all do together to make (even a small) positive impact? To begin to answer these questions, I often return to a quote in Stephen Covey's classic book, *The Seven Habits of Highly Effective People*. He wrote: "As we look at those things within our Circle of Concern, it becomes apparent that there are some things over which we have no real control and others that we can do something about. We could identify these concerns in the latter group by circumscribing them within a smaller Circle of Influence.... Proactive people focus their efforts in the Circle of Influence. They work on the things that they can do something about. The nature of their energy is positive, enlarging, and magnifying, causing their Circle of Influence to increase." That positive energy is what reinforces and energizes the ripple, which has the capacity to engulf everyone in its wake.

These ripples begin with the people in our circle of influence, the individuals in our community, even if it's only a handful of them. The individuals in our circle of influence play the determining factor in how we overcome the challenges we currently face and those that lie ahead in the future. Each ripple is like a network of individuals who, as a whole, possess all the skills, talents, and resources to thrive and make an impact. Human beings naturally depend on one another for survival. The family — loosely defined, since families are both given and chosen — is the perfect pattern for successful communities. Throughout history, people have lived in small groups or tribes, clustering together for protection, friendship, division of labor, food, and shared skills. In ancient times, banishment from the tribe or community was a certain death sentence. Yet when a group of people work together, their ability to survive significantly increases. So, too, does their ability to thrive in what psychologist Ryan M. Niemiec calls a "virtuous circle." He explains that when we observe another person express love or perform an act of kindness (or exhibit mindful awareness), this leads us to feel love or empathy. This felt sense of love or empathy then motivates us to observe our own behaviors more closely and find more opportunities for similar expressions, which leads us to be more deliberate and conscious about expressing love and empathy in the future. Niemiec writes: "This virtuous circle becomes clear: mindfulness → character strengths → mindfulness → character strengths. Each positively influencing the other." The circle is "virtuous" because, as it continues, it widens and expands positive behavior. We are influenced by others, others influence us, and eventually our ripples intersect and overlap.

There are at least three factors that converge as we commit to and focus on expanding these virtuous circles: We develop a community where all people can feel truly held and seen; we practice acceptance of human fallibility, which makes everyone feel safe; and we commit to deep collaboration, which supports truth learning and the willingness to be flexible when things don't go as planned. Expansion of our ripples requires transformation, and transformation always requires a change in our responses to a situation. We need to always remember that the ripple starts from within each of us, and thus, we must be committed to finding a path that always addresses our own needs as we continue to show up and do the work, as virtuous as it may be. Many times, we can lose ourselves in the work and get swallowed by the waves of our ripples. So this is a reminder to include our own needs in the equation — alongside, and not instead of, the communities we are seeking to serve. When we do this, we are more likely to create inclusive care for everyone.

Every time the circles expand outward, we discover the possibility of addressing the needs of more people, but we also encounter additional challenges or a need for additional steps. True virtuous circles of influence are nondiscerning. They include everyone, and we don't — and shouldn't — get to pick and choose; like a tide that rises and lifts all boats, they are all-encompassing and include all those whom we may consciously and unconsciously classify as the "other." For example, some people classify the "other" based on socioeconomic status, education, or physical ability. Some people make distinctions based on political views. In my community-building work, I am always taken aback by the willingness of individuals working toward peace, equality, and equity to leave out those who have different points of view, especially on the political spectrum. Virtuous circles of influence stem from a place of love, and therefore they cannot successfully expand outward with anger or hatred.

From what I have witnessed and experienced, most people do not include whomever they consider as the "other" in their circles of influence, and this is tragic. Without caring for those we define as the "other," without the active desire to make the world work for them as well as us, we will just end up with more division, not healing. I know it is especially challenging to include those we deem to be our "enemies," for whatever reason — whether they have wronged us personally or society at large. I struggle with this as well. Yet I recognize that we are all human, and all people can be caught up in their own suffering and traumas, which they sometimes inflict on others. Rather than spend my time making distinctions and trying to exclude certain individuals, I try to find a way to keep my heart fully open, finding enough love to bridge that gap and extend the ripple, trusting in everyone's humanity, trusting my own humanity. My virtuous circles require the strength and courage to believe in the fundamental knowledge that even the "worst of us" are just like me. Some people express their needs in unhealthy and damaging ways — in acts of violence, torture, and oppression that I cannot fathom. But I hold to the deep faith that there is no difference in the basic fabric of all of us.

When I am teaching, engaged in an act of kindness, or deep in service, I can feel the love emanating outward, and I can actively experience the (perceived) gaps dissolving. How do we work on making this feeling our immediate go-to or default mode, regardless of who or what we are facing? I lean into the phrase from *Reflections* by François de La Rochefoucauld: "We pardon to the extent that we love." I think about a world where we exhibit a completely different approach to humanity, creating a community of care where even people with blood on their hands can receive enough love to find their way back into their own hearts, so they can grieve what they have done, have true remorse and resolution, and come to belong again. Wouldn't we want that chance for ourselves? I can only imagine the healing that would occur for all of us if such a virtuous place existed.

CHAPTER TEN

Mutual Aid:
Solidarity, Not Charity

The mutual-aid tendency in man has so remote an origin,
and is so deeply interwoven with all the past evolution of the
human race, that it has been maintained by mankind up to
the present time, notwithstanding all vicissitudes of history.

— PETER KROPOTKIN

I spent much of my childhood in the neighborhoods of Jerusalem. It was quaint and crowded and full of family and rather
lovely — the sort of place and time you're desperate to leave when
you're young and full of fire and don't want to be surrounded by
so many people, but which you hanker for when you get a little
older. Back then, almost all of my aunts and uncles lived within
a few blocks of one another. I could walk up a long, winding lane
and across railroad tracks with fields on both sides to get from one
side of "town" to the other. My entire world was self-contained
within a few blocks. The doors of homes were not just always un-
locked, but they were literally always wide open. For the hours I

spent walking, sometimes alone and sometimes with my cousins, I had beautiful scenery as far as the eye could see — stone walls of an ancient city people only dream of visiting one day, historic landmarks from centuries ago, quiet streets on Shabbat (Saturdays) with almost no cars driving through them.

I quietly listened when my aunts and uncles, the elders in my life, grew nostalgic and talked to me about a magical time that existed long, long ago. This mystical dimension was called "back in the day." Back in the day, everyone knew their neighbors — I mean really knew their neighbors — so much so that if Jacob down the street lost his job, everyone in the community made sure that Jacob was able to pay his mortgage, that his children never experienced food insecurity, and that Jacob had a job interview lined up the following week. Back in the day, if Sara was diagnosed with a chronic illness, her children got rides home from school, did homework with the Cohen kids down the street, and were fed and then sent home right before bedtime, so Mom could focus on getting well. Back in the day, when someone in the community passed away, those they left behind were surrounded by a safety net of people, not just for a day or a week, but for the duration of their lives. Back in the day, people didn't feel like they were going through this life alone. The community had their back, which felt like a moral obligation.

Now, I recognize that this picture-perfect portrait is romanticized. It evokes life during a simpler time, a world before our modern technological — and even industrial — revolution. I understand that, back in the day, the fabric of society had many flaws, especially if you were a woman, a person of color, an immigrant, or a person with disabilities. But for just a moment, suspend any disbelief and imagine how we might cocreate back in the day right now, today, in this moment. Not like science-fiction time travel to another place, but to live in a world where everyone matters, where everyone can feel seen and heard, a place where every single person has something (or many things) they can offer to the world, and where every single person has something (or many things) that they need from the world. This world is possible through the simple, direct concept of mutual aid — the mutually beneficial, reciprocal exchange of goods and services — administered by communities of care. I have proof.

People sometimes quote Gandhi about the importance of the self in self-care. He famously said, "We must transform ourselves to transform the world." Of course, I agree that we must transform ourselves first, but we cannot stop at simply transforming ourselves. I think Gandhi meant this, too. Self-care and community care go hand in hand and are related. I certainly could have stopped with my inner work — tending to my own wounds and working on sustaining my physical wellness and controlling my eye disease. But personal health also depends on the health of the world, and that world also needs healing. As we practice self-care and become more aware, we don't then limit or close that aperture. Rather, our awareness widens to include others and our surroundings — so that we see the beautiful places and moments as well as the immense suffering and sadness. After returning to the cushion, I discovered that we are capable of holding both truths in duality — the good and the bad, the happiness and the sadness, the thriving and the suffering.

As I was "accidentally" building communities, expanding the ripples of my circles of influence to include anyone and everyone who would show up, I witnessed in real time the inequities that exist. I saw them up close, at a microscopic level, in a way I had never witnessed before. Of course, I knew that people struggled, but I learned about things like time poverty, gas rationing,

Wi-Fi-signal borrowing, and the need for a break from the kids. I recognized in every city that I visited, with every group that I spoke to — from high-falutin' executives at public companies to parents at Title I schools in underserved areas — that, indeed, every single human being on this planet has something that they need. But equally, every single human being on this planet has something they can offer. This fundamental truth is accurate regardless of a person's socioeconomic status, age, ability, or any other category. These fundamental truths existed in my own community of care — but as my circle of influence expanded, I recognized this on a completely different level. Further, I was learning how to build out these pillars while removing the biggest obstacle that exists when it comes to receiving help: having to ask for help. A formalized structure of mutual aid directly addresses this problem and is a pillar of every formalized community of care.

As my weekly gatherings at the beach continued to grow, I got to know the "regulars" and the people they cared about. I learned about happy occasions, of course, but many of the people who waited to speak to me after meditation class ended shared stories of loss — suffering and struggle that were both tangible and ambiguous. In each case, I tried to practice mutual aid. For example: If someone told me about their financial woes because they lost their job, I immediately connected them to someone else on the beach who was a business owner looking to hire people. To take it a step further, if the individual also had no savings and was worried about paying rent on time and putting food in the fridge, I would quietly start a collection circle and crowdfund enough money to help them until they were gainfully employed again. The gesture was automatic. Another example: When an elderly woman with cataracts could no longer drive to meditation class — I had noticed she had stopped coming on Sunday and inquired about her — I was able to find someone who lived in her area who was happy to pick her up and drive her to the beach on Sunday mornings. Both women benefited tremendously from this interaction. I have hundreds, maybe even thousands, of similar examples over the years of this direct mutual aid. It was inherently understood that here, in *my* community of care, we took care of one another at all costs.

During certain times of year, like during back-to-school months or the holiday season, we amplified our mutual-aid efforts and made it incredibly easy for folks to ask for what they needed and for a redistribution of wealth to occur. I define the term *wealth* loosely; it doesn't exclusively mean money. We can be wealthy in different, concurrent ways — in health, time, energy, and so on. Thus, on a macro level, mutual aid can work through the transference of capital but on a more local, microcommunity level, it can include things like an exchange of goods and services, lending a hand or an ear, or spending time with someone. It means converging "back in the day" and the classifieds section of a newspaper so that all needs are met and anyone with any form of wealth can find a place or person to gift it to. This redistribution of wealth happens without any bureaucracy or overhead; it is direct. It can also be scaled up during times when the community-at-large is suffering through a hurricane, a wildfire, or any other tragedy on a massive scale. When local community-of-care structures are in place and everyone's circles of influence expand outward to others in the community — and overlap with other communities of care — the creation of a mutual-aid network that permeates every level of the community is achievable. We can attain communities where everyone's needs are met and everyone can offer help.

For example, when Hurricane Dorian hit the Bahamas in

September 2019, our microcommunity — a little less than two hundred miles away from the hardest hit islands in the Caribbean — was already poised and ready to mobilize and help. Our structure of giving was in place; our community members already knew how to mobilize and expand their giving circles beyond just our own community. As the eye of the Category 5 storm hovered over the Bahamas, leaders from our community were already plotting and planning reconnaissance efforts, organizing supply drives, and securing transport by plane and by sea to the outer islands that would have the greatest need for support and relief. We were already built for it. We were ready. In the aftermath, our efforts continued to expand as we merged with other similar groups in the region. As everyone divided and conquered, our overlapping efforts became even more efficient, impactful, and responsive. Here is what overlapping mutual-aid communities look like:

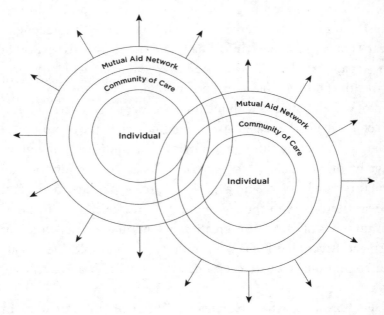

Pandemic of Love:
How Mutual Aid Can Respond to Crisis

In 2020, in the thick of the global Covid-19 pandemic, New York congresswoman Alexandria Ocasio-Cortez tweeted about mutual aid, and mutual-aid workshops began popping up on Zoom platforms, and *The New York Times* did a piece on the existence of mutual-aid networks in major cities. The slogan for mutual aid is "social solidarity, not charity," but the simplicity of that message doesn't necessarily do a good job of explaining what that means, nor does it provide a road map for achieving it. In its simplest terms, mutual aid builds simple and direct structures of cooperation that eliminate or reduce the need for reliance on the government, charitable organizations, or philanthropists to address a community's needs. We live in a society that is riddled with top-down approaches, complex infrastructures, and indirect solutions that are wasteful and inefficient. Mutual aid creates horizontal solidarity networks that flow in every direction, not only from the top down.

The ideas and practice of mutual aid date back to the turn of the twentieth century. Its origins are rooted in late-nineteenth-century naturalist debates and the earliest theories of anarchist socialism. The birth of the idea of mutual aid itself is associated with the popular Russian anarchist-socialist thinker Peter Kropotkin. He was a globally revered naturalist, geographer, and advocate of scientific thought. In the late 1800s, in response to the profound impact of Charles Darwin's theory of evolution, Kropotkin (along with other Russian scientists) developed mutual aid as a competitive theory, especially in the space of social science. The well-known Darwinian concept "survival of the fittest," when applied to humans, is most often used to justify things like war, violence, and destruction — with the underlying belief that humans are the "fittest" of all species and that within our species there is a further hierarchy of fitness. The application of Darwinian theory as a social theory, and not just a biological one, was popularized by social scientist and biologist Herbert Spencer. Spencer believed that human societies, like organisms, could also evolve progressively. Kropotkin was deeply concerned about this interpretation of evolutionary theory because he worried that the social applications of "survival of the fittest" would be used to justify poverty, colonialism, gender inequality, racism, casteism, and war. His premonitions were right, and in the decades and centuries that followed, people have indeed justified these inequities as "natural," innate, and even immutable expressions of our very genetic being.

In this dangerous line of thinking, casteism and capitalism are viewed merely as "natural" competition on a neutral playing field, one that eventually produces winners and losers based on merit or "fitness" and nothing more. Yet those who insist that any individual can "pull themselves up by their bootstraps" overlook the fact that many people have no boots in the first place. Kropotkin chose instead to focus on the opposite of competition — cooperation. Taking examples from nature, he showed how groups of species work together to not only survive but thrive: wolf packs, ant colonies, the pollination process between bees and flowers, and human clans. His argument was that, while competition exists, so, too, does cooperation, and each should be examined equally. In his 1902 book *Mutual Aid: A Factor in Evolution*, Kropotkin put forth that "the fittest are not the physically strongest, nor the cunningest, but those who learn to combine so as mutually to support each other, strong and weak alike, for the welfare of the community."

Today, mutual aid exists in innovative organizations and uses processes that connect worldwide movements with hyper-local communities. In March 2020, when the coronavirus led to state-by-state shelter-in-home orders in the United States, I found myself, like everyone else the world over, distressed, afraid of the unknown, and filled with anxiety. Meditation teachers are not immune to those feelings, but they have developed the tools to deal with them. As I was scrolling through my social media feeds, reading emails, and sending text messages to check on the most vulnerable in our community, I leaned into the default mode that I often spoke about on Sunday mornings: cultivating love over fear. I asked myself: What can I do right now, *in this moment*, to extend a safety net for our community, bring people together in a time of isolation, and provide hope?

Having used a variety of mutual-aid models, informal and formal, within our community and while helping others, I knew that our members would easily adopt this structure. As I describe in chapter 9 (see "Drop a Pebble, Start a Ripple," page 147), I created two simple forms online, entitled "Give Help" and "Get Help," which community members could fill out, and then I planned to connect people in need with those who could fulfill that need. Along with a short video, here is what I posted to my social media accounts:

> Announcing a #pandemicoflove, a tangible way to support or help others in our community: I've been really worried about a lot of people in our community who are hurting. So many of you work in jobs that get paid hourly wages, count on tips, are in the hospitality and event industry, and beyond.... I've put together a system for our community to help each other — we have people who need help and people

who are in a privileged situation that can afford to help those in need. For those in need, you can confidentially fill out the Request for Assistance form and request the help you need (example: grocery bills, utility bills, medicine costs, gas, etc.). For those in a position to help a specific community member or family, you can indicate the quantity and frequency with which you can help on the Love a Community Member form. Over the next few days I will privately connect those with a need with a person who can help fill that need. Please feel free to share these forms. This is our time to come together and shine, to rise up, to show up and love one another. I am here to support each of you in your time of need and hope to see you virtually on Sunday morning when we come together as a community to meditate and alleviate suffering as one.

As I described earlier, I was stunned by the response. Hundreds upon hundreds of people signed up on both forms, and hundreds of people were sharing the post on their own social media. As I started to dig in and match individuals in need with patrons who could fill their needs, I soon realized I needed help. I was barely making a dent because the entries were growing at a faster rate than I could match people. So I turned to several friends and local community members whom I knew had some time on their hands and could help me.

Our volunteer network grew quickly as people joined in and sought help replicating this model in their own communities. Within the first week, Pandemic of Love mutual-aid efforts had begun in San Francisco, Seattle, Chicago, Lisbon, and Barcelona, to name a few. Using Zoom, I trained each new chapter, providing lessons learned and best practices and sharing the knowledge our South Florida team was amassing in real time. Within a month, dozens of #pandemicoflove chapter cities existed in the United States, and within two months, there was a global network of hundreds of volunteers, a weekly Zoom gathering, and a What'sApp group chat between everyone. We had the attention of influencers and the media; we were conduits responsible for the direct transaction of what became millions of dollars. We were providing people everywhere with hope and proving that the need for connection is deeply seated in humanity. We were proving with each match that diseases are not the only thing that can go viral. Love, hope, and kindness can be infectious, too.

I think that the most incredible revelation for me in these moments of fear and isolation is precisely what Kropotkin focused on — how deeply connected humans are and how much we need to collaborate with one another. The success and growth of Pandemic of Love proved that mutual aid goes beyond charity by mobilizing humans on behalf of humanity. It provides us with a powerful vision of the type of alternative society that is possible, one where we can be a global community connected by cooperative compassion and where we are no longer consumers in endless capitalist competition.

Like Pandemic of Love, tens of thousands of other Covid-19 mutual-aid groups cropped up throughout the country and around the globe in 2020 and 2021 as people created the cooperative community structures that have existed since the dawn of humanity. Many of these groups were formed by neighbors who came together to do things like deliver groceries and prescriptions for those who were self-isolating, assist with the payment of bills, and even make phone calls to those who were living alone or who needed extra moral support. While I already knew, based on our own South Florida community, that mutual-aid structures could work on a local level, what Pandemic of Love proved to me is that we can build alternative social relationships on a larger scale and completely shift the dominant idea of how society is "supposed" to work. There is a better, more efficient, and more compassionate way to exist that can also shift political culture.

The UK-based organization Covid-19 Mutual Aid UK (covid mutualaid.org) beautifully summarizes this potential on its website:

> Mutual aid is where a group of people organize to meet their own needs, outside of the formal frameworks of charities, NGOs, and government. It is, by definition, a horizontal mode of organizing, in which all individuals are equally powerful. There are no "leaders" or elected "steering committees" in mutual-aid projects; there is only a group of people who work together as equals. Mutual aid isn't about "saving" anyone; it's about people coming together, in a spirit of solidarity, to support and look out for one another.

As I compare the scale of Pandemic of Love chapters versus local, formal communities of care, I think there are pros and cons to each. During large-scale events like natural disasters and pandemics, having a larger infrastructure and casting a wide net to attract donors is especially important. However, on a day-to-day basis, smaller is better. Someone's personal community of care can easily create a formalized mutual-aid microcommunity, and when needed, this can scale up and join forces with other microcommunities to amplify impact. In smaller communities, participants get to know the needs of each member and of the area in general, while facilitating relationships and true connection. I think it is easier to establish trust at a more local level, which is important because mutual aid depends upon people admitting to vulnerability and accepting help from strangers. Knowing someone is in your geographic area can help to moderate this fear.

Eliminating the Fear of Asking for Help

Mutual aid makes it easier to ask for help by sometimes even eliminating the need to make a formal request. The "back in the day" model inherently assumes that community members are plugged in to everyone's needs on a granular level — so that they know how or when to offer assistance even if someone in need doesn't make a formal ask. This is an incredibly important piece of the puzzle as we move toward building out communities where everyone feels safe, seen, and heard. The success of mutual-aid models is proof that human beings are inherently social and need to be interconnected. However, society conditions us to believe exactly the opposite, particularly in individualistic Western cultures. Many of us are raised with the belief that reliance on others is a burden and that asking for help implies weakness and insufficiency. What is incredibly ironic about these deeply ingrained beliefs is that not a single person on this planet has fully "succeeded" on their own without the help of others. It's not wrong to prize independence, but we can't forget that we depend on others just as much if not more. The two must be in balance.

In fact, asking for help requires us to be resourceful, which is a key element of emotional strength. If everyone starts with the premise that humans naturally evolved to be interdependent, we make it possible for each individual to be comfortable enough to feel vulnerable and courageous enough to admit when they need help. This helps each individual in the community to openly and genuinely acknowledge their specific needs and limitations, as well as their unique skills, talents, and resources — and to understand that *everyone* has both. By formally acknowledging this in our communities of care, followed by formally identifying both sides of the give-receive equation, it becomes easier to ask for help. It normalizes the fact that we are independent *and* interdependent beings. If we allow ourselves to rely on one another and to experience our needs and limitations, this makes us emotionally strong individually and emotionally strong collectively.

Asking for help is neither a burden nor a sign of weakness; it's a sign of being human. The same is true of larger societal problems in the areas of health care, inequity, unemployment, housing, and food insecurity. These are human issues, and when we strengthen human relationships, these issues are no longer experienced as abstract societal issues, but as local realities that affect someone we personally know. When we directly witness and experience the impact these seemingly abstract issues have on the lives of people we know, social transformation can occur. True human connection requires us to be willing to walk a mile in someone else's shoes, to view the world through their lens for even a few moments. It means connecting at the heart center, tapping into our empathy, and recognizing that our actions and words can directly affect the life of another human being. It reminds us that we are not alone, that we have never been alone, and that we will never be alone. This vision is captured by activist Yashna Padamsee: "I cannot sit and care for my body without being concerned with what happens to the bodies of my brothers and sisters. We are connected....It is our responsibility, not as individuals, but as communities to create structures in which self-care changes to community care. In which we are cared for and able to care for others."

Reflecting back now on my personal moments of immense

suffering after my divorce and during the onset of my eye disease, I feel an incredible amount of gratitude. I had friends and family who stepped in to informally become my community. I realize that not everyone has a community, let alone even one person, they can count on to step up and help them. In my situation, my village showed up for me even when I didn't ask for help — and I seldom did ask at the beginning. I didn't want to be a burden or to be the subject of anyone's "pity party." In situations where a person doesn't have that built-in village or community, or even a single support buddy, having a formalized mutual-aid network in place not only provides a safety net but also greatly decreases the anxiety and shame related to asking for help. That's because the recipient is also a donor. In a mutual-aid network based on a reciprocal exchange of goods and services, everyone in the community has something they need and something to offer; everyone both gives and receives. When I think about this kind of symbiotic ecosystem, I can't think of anyone better than Tess to illustrate the point.

Tess was an early sand tribe attendee. She joined the community within the first three months after we started gathering. Tess was a small-in-stature-but-big-in-personality woman in her forties, single and a lover of the ocean. She was the type of person whom you couldn't help but immediately be drawn to with her warm smile, sparkling eyes, and long flowing hair. One Sunday morning after meditation ended and people were dispersing, Tess approached me as I was packing up my towel. She grabbed both of my hands and looked me square in the eyes. "I need to tell you something important," she said in an uncharacteristic tone.

"Sure, of course," I said. "What's going on?"

"Well" — she paused to take a breath — "I was diagnosed last week with breast cancer. It's somewhat advanced, but I am looking at all of my options and will need to take time off of work to start getting treatments." I leaned in to hug her; no words needed to be spoken. I unrolled my towel on the sand, and Tess and I sat down to speak about the logistics of the treatment and what her needs were. However, she was so overwhelmed that she couldn't wrap her head around what she needed at that point. She promised to get back to me and insisted that, for now, she really had it all covered.

Our community didn't wait for Tess to get back to us; she was a member of our mutual-aid ecosystem, which meant that we had an obligation to make sure she had that safety net and that her needs were met so she could focus on the biggest battle of her life. Her community immediately created a fundraiser and ensured that she always had warm meals and a ride to her appointments and to the beach when the going got tough. Tess — being, well, Tess — had "paid into the system" for years. She had helped to spearhead relief drives when natural disasters struck; she had mobilized to help single mothers of children with special needs and to make sure that our canine and feline community members had their veterinary bills taken care of. When, directly or indirectly, she heard about a problem, a gap, or a concern, she would get to work to fulfill the need herself or find the person in our community who had the resources to do it. Even after she learned about the community's formalized efforts to help her, Tess continued to do her share by forming an official group called the "Sand Tribe Cancer Support Group" to provide moral support to community members who were either actively dealing with the disease or survivors. I am proud of the fact that Tess never felt ashamed to ask for help when she needed it, though sadly this wound up being the final year of her life. The community always had her back, and Tess always had ours.

Setting Up Your Own Mutual-Aid Network

Mutual aid is a complex, emergent process that operates on a local scale and is based on the strength of relationships. In order to set up your own mutual-aid network, the first thing to do is to develop a core team. This can be the same group of people who make up your community of care, it can be a subset of it, or it can be a combination of several communities of care that are geographically close. Organizing requires spending a lot of time together, so think about people you trust and who are committed to showing up. Start by gathering one or two other trusted people who are plugged in to your community's needs and can help you brainstorm and make connections. Once you better define all the needs of your community — is it food, access to health care, assistance with forms and programs? — reach out to a small circle of between five to twenty people who are interested in forming a mutual-aid network. I learned this the hard way.

Within the first week of starting Pandemic of Love, dozens of people reached out to ask how they could replicate the model in their own community. I spoke to each person to learn more and to vet them, and then I replicated our forms and provided them with access to links and with training and support. Initially, I did this for anyone who reached out, even if it was just one person, but I learned quickly that starting a new community with only one person was a mistake. I experienced this myself as the demand for help grew daily and new donors poured in. Managing a mutual-aid community alone was an impossible task, and I enlisted a half-dozen volunteers within the first week of launching. So thinking that someone in a different community could manage everything alone was a mistake.

In the early days, our chapter leaders met regularly in virtual conference rooms, and we shared best practices. We quickly realized that, generally speaking, the chapters that started up with at least five volunteers were the most efficient, sustainable, and successful. As is true for all self-care, you cannot pour from an empty cup, and one or two people cannot sustain the level of management and compassion required to manage a mutual-aid community (especially in the midst of a crisis). Therefore, the most important thing you can do before you even get started is to create a network.

When considering who to include in your network, it's incredibly useful to draw a pod map. A pod map is a really simple tool that can help you remember all the people you are connected to, and in turn, all the people they are connected to. These do not have to all be individuals you know deeply, but rather, they can be acquaintances or organizations with the capacity and bandwidth to be of service and who, in turn, may need help with something themselves. The idea is that you deepen these relationships as you continue to work together. The key is to clearly identify a geographic support area before you begin reaching out to others to make connections. Your area could be people in your building; on your block; in your church, synagogue, or mosque; in your yoga class; or in your book club. The question you need to answer is: Who are you trying to support? To make connections, ask questions to discover the needs and abilities of the community you are trying to support. Questions can be super straightforward: What are your needs? What do you need help with? Or you can get right to the heart of the matter by asking for a list of the most pressing financial constraints (such as specific bills) or which one task, errand, or chore would alleviate the biggest headache.

It is also critical to build on existing networks in your defined area. A number of organizations may already be servicing, in one capacity or another, underserved and vulnerable populations. Reach out to form bridges, alliances, and feeder systems that fulfill both sides of the mutual-aid equation. This helps to build a solid foundation and provides credibility and a boost to a newly formed community. For example, the Seattle-based mutual-aid network Big Door Brigade has links to a wide range of community providers, and because of those relationships, they are able to offer things like legal support and bail funds, housing, and childcare. Then, throughout the process of building the organization, and once it has become established, continue to consistently communicate in person and on a one-on-one basis to deepen the relationships with each individual in the pod. Broadcasting communications — through emails, video conferencing with the entire community, social media, and even messaging platforms like WhatsApp or Slack — can only go so far. Mutual aid is not about transactions; it's about relationships. The cohesion of the network is strengthened and motivates people to continue to be plugged in when these relationships are reinforced consistently.

Finally, a word to the wise: Mutual-aid organizations are not static. Rather, they are breathing, living organisms that need to be adaptive, flexible, and responsive to the community's changing needs. It is important not to get bogged down in a standardized structure or model, but to continuously evaluate what is needed, where there are gaps, and where there can be even more efficiency. Remember, unlike traditional charitable organizations, the goal of mutual aid is not to bog the process down with bureaucratic red tape. The goal is to keep things flowing and direct. Also, while the concept of mutual aid is a timeless principle, it doesn't mean it cannot be continuously improved upon, especially with the advent of new and improving technology.

The proactive formation and existence of mutual-aid networks prepares a community for any crisis it may face. The model is scalable in both directions: It can grow bigger when needed and stay hyper-local in times of more stability. Mutual aid empowers community members to shape their own futures, helping to provide order and infrastructure to create the type of world we all want to live in.

Mutual aid does not need to be a temporary fix that arises only in times of crisis. I contend that it can be a new way of life — and in many ways, a return to life as it was "back in the day." In her book *A Paradise Built in Hell: The Extraordinary Communities That Arise in Disaster*, Rebecca Solnit points to the "improvised, collaborative, cooperative, and local society" that can emerge after devastating natural disasters that require community rebuilding. She writes:

> This is a paradise of rising to the occasion that points out by contrast how the rest of the time most of us fall down from the heights of possibility, down into diminished selves and dismal societies. Many now do not even hope for a better society, but they recognize it when they encounter it, and that discovery shines out even through the namelessness of their experience. Others recognize it, grasp it, and make something of it, and long-term social and political transformations, both good and bad, arise from the wreckage. The door to this era's potential paradises is in hell.

Many organizations that are now established institutions were born out of a response to times of crisis. For example, the International Red Cross, one of the oldest humanitarian organizations, was formed to take care of the casualties of war. The Catholic Church developed a health-care system and built hospitals in the

United States in response to pandemics such as cholera and the 1918 Spanish flu. What these lasting institutions and structures — from unions to charities — realized is that the needs revealed in a crisis usually existed long before the crisis began, and they need to be met long after the crisis is over. As Solnit points out, "It's tempting to ask why, if you fed your neighbors during the time of the earthquake and fire, you didn't do so before or after." As we seek to create societies that serve the needs of *all people*, we need to build sustainable infrastructures that create equity and true community. Formalized mutual aid is an important pillar in that vision.

PART THREE

RISE UP

[The Movement to Us]

CHAPTER ELEVEN

Enough Is a Feast

He who knows that enough is enough
will always have enough.

— LAO-TZU

As I've said, by the end of 2015, by most conventional measures, my life was going pretty well with little to complain about in the grand scheme of things. I had great friends and family, a good job, and a roof over my head, and I certainly knew where my next meals were coming from. My eye disease was manageable, and I had access to the best care and treatment options available to me. In fact, to this day, my eye issues remain an ongoing battle; while I can still see, the slow, progressive deterioration in my sight now means I am considered visually impaired.

However, accumulating more in my life — more material possessions, more commitments, more meetings, more financial responsibilities, more hassle — wasn't making me feel happier. Alongside all this accumulation, I felt like less and less of my time was, well — *my* time. I was rich in "stuff" but experiencing massive time poverty.

Then, as now, I want to live in a world guided by the premise that enough is a feast. I want to live in a world with true equity, where structures such as mutual aid are not only formalized but institutionalized in every community around the country and throughout the world. I want to live in a world where helping someone meet a need isn't seen as a handout. Rather, it embodies a spirit of empathy, generosity, and dignity. When we engage in mutual aid, we gift one another with the beginnings of a new world, premised on reciprocal, voluntaristic, and egalitarian social relations. We make sure that everyone on this Earth has enough because certainly the Earth's bounty has proven time and again that there is more than enough for everyone. Enough is all we need. We are collectively self-determining and self-organizing, and we can self-govern in ways that supply everyone with what they need as well as what they desire, all while weaving beloved webs of communities of care.

In our own lives, we often complain that we never have enough time or money; we take on too many commitments and obligations; we live a cluttered life in a cluttered house with a cluttered calendar. Yet when we learn to shed the extra "stuff," we enhance the quality of our lives. Simplifying our lives actually gives us the space to *live* our lives and, more importantly, to *give* the excess to others so we can balance the scales and make the world more equitable. Society seems to pull us in two directions simultaneously — we pursue contentment and relaxation while also remaining driven, which keeps us stressed. We strive to avoid pain or "bad" feelings while we accumulate honors and recognitions, accolades, stuff, and the validation of others. It's a vicious cycle that keeps us in a rat race and fuels the industrial wellness complex that currently exists. But to what end? Comedian Lily Tomlin put it perfectly when she said, "If you are in a rat race and you win, you are still a rat."

Why are we in this constant pursuit for fulfillment and happiness? There are many reasons, but the most important ones relate to evolution. Humans, like all animals, adapted in ways that helped them to survive, which primarily depended upon avoiding harm at all costs. Those strategies, efforts, and abilities that improved survival were passed on to each generation, which developed them further. In essence, individuals who were driven, anxious, and cooperative with others were more likely to survive.

Every day we are inundated with constant messages and images that tell us that we need more stuff. Even if we avoided all media — unplugging our social media feeds and the television, disconnecting from the internet — society would still condition us to value individualism and to correlate self-worth with things like wealth, accomplishments, title, and appearance. In this particular race, there is no winning: The "finish line" keeps moving, so that no matter what we achieve, it's never enough for long. We keep expecting, and are expected, to do more.

Another impact of evolution is how memory works. We are wired to remember painful experiences more vividly, like pain, loss, shame, grief, and anxiety. Meanwhile, good or pleasurable memories aren't remembered as vividly. The reason, of course, is that, in order to survive, it's much more important to remember harmful experiences in order to avoid them in the future. I once heard a psychologist at a meditation retreat describe it this way: We have Velcro for pain, but Teflon for pleasure.

Furthermore, our brains turn entire experiences into singular, stable moments — in essence, turning verbs into nouns. The term for this is *cognitive essentializing*. That is, when we see, smell, taste, touch, or hear something that we associate with an event, we are reminded of the experience of that event. And we can try to hold on to experiences we like and enjoy by repeating the sensations we associate with them, but this is an exercise in futility. Those experiences slip through the cracks; it is impossible to bottle contentment and happiness. Yet we keep reaching for that next hit of dopamine, that positive hormone, as fleeting as it is, in part because we evolved to be anxious creatures who are always striving for more. Then we are further conditioned by nurture, by society, to want to get ahead, to believe we are broken and must be fixed. We can become like children trying to capture happy moments like fireflies in a mason jar. Yet like fireflies, those feelings are inherently ephemeral, and trying to capture and preserve them is fruitless.

There Is Enough for Everyone

A lot of the inspiration for my own work is steeped in the movements inspired by one person throughout history. For me, all roads lead back to Mohandas Gandhi, the Indian political activist who revolutionized the world with his thoughts and actions. Gandhi lived from 1869 until 1948, and he devoted his life to seeking truth in so many areas of interest, such as social justice, political justice, and economic justice. I think it would be accurate to describe Gandhi as a minimalist, someone who owned very few possessions. Many of his essays and talks expressed his belief that each person on this planet only needs enough to meet their basic needs, and that if each person were to adhere to this fundamental principle, every human could be provided with what they need to survive. That is, with enough. One of his most famous quotes is "Earth provides enough to satisfy every man's need, but not every man's greed."

All we need to do is look around to see that the world we live in is unbalanced — there are those who live in excess and those who are struggling and scraping by to survive. In that excess, there is wastefulness; enormous wealth coexists with incredible poverty. Gandhi often spoke about the need for a redistribution of wealth, how those who have their needs more than met should voluntarily give the excess away to those whose needs are not met. Of course, Gandhi was critical of capitalism and advocated for a system that measured national wealth beyond the GDP, a standard that is misleading and immoral. Standards of wealth should include quality of life. In other words, true wealth isn't measured by the number of millionaires in a country but by the absence of homelessness and starvation.

Gandhi was greatly influenced by John Ruskin's book *Unto This Last*, which was written in 1860. In her book *Conquest of Violence: The Gandhian Philosophy of Conflict*, Joan Bondurant says that Ruskin's ideas could be boiled down to three principles: First, that the good of an individual is contained in the good of all; second, that a lawyer, barber, and janitor all have equal value, earning their livelihood from their work; and third, that a life of labor is a life worth living. In fact, Gandhi published a translation of Ruskin's book, which he aptly titled *Sarvodaya*, which is a Sanskrit word meaning "the welfare of all." For both Ruskin and Gandhi, the possession of wealth morally requires an equitable redistribution that protects the core of human dignity, making the wealthy the "trustees" of the common good. Gandhi viewed poverty as "the worst form of violence"; by that he meant that it's barbaric if someone has it in their power to alleviate the suffering of another but instead chooses to spend their wealth frivolously.

These ideas are what lead me to define the word *wealth* broadly. Quality of life is determined by more than someone's bank account, and any discussion of creating a more equitable society involving the redistribution of wealth should discuss more than money. What makes us wealthy? The people I know and talk to say many things: being in good health, the ability to have free time, the liberty to choose how to spend that time, and having a community of friends and family we can count on, to name a few. When we evaluate our lives using this expanded definition of wealth, it's clear that we all have some wealth and something valuable to contribute to the world, to our community, to one another. If, as Gandhi believed, we all have a moral responsibility to give in the areas where we have excess, then we all can be involved in cocreating the world we want to live in. We can collectively build a new infrastructure together, where everyone can help advance a vision of equity. We all are stakeholders in the movement. We all have an important part to play.

In today's climate, how can we enact some of the principles and practices that Gandhi espoused almost a century ago? First, we need to emulate the sentiment of his bold statement, "My life is my message." Gandhi put his money where his mouth is (pun intended). We need to practice what we preach and not just expect "someone else" to take care of atrocity, injustice, and inequity. At a protest a few years ago, I saw a woman holding a sign that read: "I used to wish that somebody would speak up, and then I realized that I am somebody." We are all somebodies. Second, Gandhi never intended to start a global movement of nonviolence. He simply made nonviolence a central principle around every activity he engaged in. His actions began directly with his own life and then expanded to his local community. He did not set out to change the world; he set out to change his community, after he refined himself. Just as the poet William Blake famously hoped "to see a world in a grain of sand and heaven in a wildflower," we need to be able to understand how we can be "small" and impactful, and how global actions can also impact us very personally.

For everyone to have enough, we need to lean into love over fear and strengthen that muscle, making that our default mode. When we are afraid of something or someone, we need to simply ask: How can I approach this from a place of love? In other words, even if we feel threatened, we can lean into a situation and use it to empower ourselves to do something rooted in love. When rooted in love, even a small action — like when I created two simple forms online when the pandemic started — can help us feel like we are doing something instead of being in a fight-flight-freeze mode. People often ask, and rightly so, how can we come from a place of love if we are being threatened? How can we reach out to help someone who is indirectly or — even worse — directly harming us? It isn't always easy, but we have to remember the principle that equity needs to include *everyone*, even the people we don't particularly like, those we vehemently abhor, and those we believe to be a threat.

While the coronavirus pandemic was going on, political divides were showing up in a variety of ways. Some of our Pandemic of Love volunteers and many of our donors, especially in the months leading up to the 2020 presidential election, resisted helping someone on the "other side" of the political spectrum. When I could convince the individual to lean into love and give anyway, the outcomes gave all parties involved hope that unity is possible. A perfect example of this was when, in late spring 2020, a Pandemic of Love volunteer assigned a self-described liberal hippie from New York, Eileen, to a conservative, pro-MAGA movement single mom, Christine, from Alabama. Eileen happened to be a member of our sand tribe meditation community, and when she found out that she was matched with someone who was, as she put it, "directly harming her," she called me to insist that she needed to be reassigned. I listened to Eileen passionately explain to me all the reasons why this individual was undeserving of help. When she finally paused, I asked her what it would look like if she approached this issue from a place of love instead of fear. For instance, in our guided meditations on the beach, we practiced a loving-kindness meditation while repeating phrases like "May you be happy, may you be free from suffering, may you be healthy," and so on, while thinking of a person we love, a person we don't know well, and a person we have difficulty with. I asked Eileen: What would it look like to take "meditation off the cushion" and not just wish for a person's suffering to end but to actually have a hand in it? If she abandoned Christine after one conversation, would she be confirming and reinforcing for Christine everything that she might think about a woman like Eileen — a liberal New York Jew? Eileen took my questions to heart and told me she would think about it and get back to me. I didn't hear from Eileen again until months later, a few weeks before the presidential election. Here is the email she sent:

Dear Shelly,

I am writing to tell you about my incredible experience with Christine, the woman I was matched with in Alabama. Originally, as you know, I was really upset that I, a liberal and feminist New Yorker who has spent my whole life working for equality and justice, was matched with a woman from the South who would think of me as nothing more than a Yankee.

I decided to call her anyway, figuring that perhaps she won't live up to the narrative I have of a single mother in Alabama living in a trailer. You teach us through your meditations to open our hearts and to have nonjudgment, and so I figured I should do that in real life, not just in my mind when meditating.

So I called her and she was EXACTLY what I thought she would be. A fervent Trump supporter (yes, I went there!!!) and someone who stood for everything that I have fought against my entire life — a racist, an anti-Semite, a white supremacist!

After our conversation I did not want to give her any help for her groceries … but then I started to think about what Michelle Obama (whom I admire greatly) said — that when "they go low, we go high." And so I mustered up all of my wits and energy, and I thought, if I don't help her, I will confirm EVERYTHING she thinks about a snowflake from the city, but if I help her, I may help to create a bridge or shift her thinking about it. I was certain she had probably never run into anyone like me before.

So nauseous as it made me, I reached out to her again and told her that I would be emailing her a gift card to Walmart biweekly for her groceries, so she and her children would be able to have food and the essentials they needed during quarantine. She was incredibly appreciative, and I wound up lightening up a little, so I asked her about her children, and she told me all about her daughter and son, ten and eight respectively. I asked her what they liked to do — and I was taken aback when she said that her son likes sports but her daughter likes to read, and "she doesn't know where she gets that from."

I knew this was my "Trojan horse" moment, and so I asked her if I could ship her daughter some age-appropriate books. She said her daughter would love that — and so I proceeded to send her a dozen books that all had a strong message of equality, social justice, diversity, and inclusion, and that would hopefully expand her world beyond the trailer park in Mobile where she was living.

Fast-forward, Christine and I speak every other week at least. She has sent me photos of her kids and texts. Her daughter loved the books I sent her, and now I am sending her more! And I still help her with groceries biweekly. Dare I say it, we have even become friends?!?

Do we talk about politics? Sure. I have told her about my family's history in the Holocaust, and I have talked to her about my work prior to retirement in New York in social justice and in the gay pride movement. She actually has a lot of liberal views (for example, she has "no issue with gay people, they can love who they want to so long as they don't bother me"), but she doesn't understand the connection between many of her views and the services she relies on (food stamps, for example) and the Democratic Party. It's actually shocking to me — not that she thinks this way, but how far removed I am and how long I have been living in a bubble, too. How many Christines could we have reached out to and connected with?

I am writing to you because this "random" connection has created a shift in me, in an old Jewish woman who thought she was too old to shift!

I never thought I would be friends with someone who had voted for Trump. And here we are. I have hopes I can sway her to vote differently in November, and I won't give up trying ... but I have decided I will help her even if she doesn't. She is a victim of the systems of government as well — a cycle

of poverty and education. I hope her son and daughter find
their way out.

    With all my love,
    Eileen

Decades before Eileen's lean-into-love experience, I had my own. I was studying abroad at the Hebrew University in Jerusalem during my junior year in college. I was still very much an observant Jew, and I was reeling from the years of terrorist bombings in Israel coupled with the rhetoric that I had heard my entire life — and very much believed — about our "enemies" across the border. I remember growing up and being so afraid every time I heard someone speaking Arabic. I was told not to get into a taxicab with a Palestinian and not to walk through Palestinian neighborhoods. The fear-based narrative in my mind associated with anyone who looked like, reminded me of, or sounded like a Palestinian was so real to me, so triggering, that you would think I had actually been attacked or hurt or even personally insulted by a Palestinian. Then when I was at Hebrew University, I had the opportunity to intern with a United Nations agency that was doing polling work and research in the Palestinian territories across Israel. I knew that I would be working with an international team and going into "forbidden" places like Hebron, Gaza, and Ramallah. Although I was terrified, I was equally intrigued and rebellious; I felt that I would be safe with the teams I would be working with. The first week, I was assigned to intern with a team led by a Swiss psychologist, a South African epidemiologist, and an Irish social worker. We were going to be conducting in-depth surveys with Palestinian mothers and discussing health conditions, food insecurity, water scarcity, and other potential human rights violations.

I remember driving for the first time through a Palestinian village, immediately recognizing the vast differences between their community and even the most underserved Israeli community just miles away. Our first stop was a building that I wouldn't have assumed anyone was even living in. It was part construction site, part demolition zone. We walked through an unlatched, squeaky iron gate and along a narrow path of limestone to arrive at a wooden door on the bottom floor, standing outside in an entryway that smelled and looked clean. A planter filled with blooming flowers made me stop and think that whoever lived here really took pride in their home and hadn't forgotten about the beauty in the world, amid all its ugliness. Derek — the Swiss psychologist — knocked on the door, and a delicate and wholesome woman named Fatima opened the door just wide enough for her head to peek through and see who was there. A few children's heads peered around her dress through the gap between her thigh and the doorway. Ahmad, our translator, exchanged a few words with her, and she opened the door wide enough to let us in, shooing the children away.

The house was small and sparse, with just the essential furnishings and barely anything hung on the walls. We were shown to the couch, and Roberta — the Irish team member who spoke fluent Arabic — turned to me and asked if I wanted some hot tea, since Fatima was going to prepare some for us. I nodded yes, distracted by a photo of Yasser Arafat, then the chairman of the Palestine Liberation Army. My heart beat faster, and I could feel the blood start to rush to my feet when suddenly a little hand tugged at my skirt. It was a little girl, her hair in a lopsided ponytail on top of her head, with big brown eyes gazing up at me and motioning for me to look at the doll in her hand. She reminded me so much of my cousin's daughter in Jerusalem, and I instantly forgot that I was frightened as I started reaching for the doll, striving to have a conversation with her as if she could understand a word I was saying. We still managed to communicate, as she pointed out the doll's hair and gestured for me to braid it. And braid it I did. Soon her younger brother arrived with a little toy car, competing for my attention. I was so engaged in my newly formed friendships that I was almost surprised when Fatima came back with a tray of glass teacups filled with hot water and mint leaves. I'd almost forgotten why I was there.

Derek and Roberta, via the translator, asked Fatima questions about her husband's recent arrest, her current living situation, and access to food, water, and education for her children. As the answers were translated back, it occurred to me that this woman wanted the same things for her children that every mother wants: She wanted them to be healthy and happy and have access to opportunities to live an easier life than she was living. As I sat in a living room in Ramallah across from my "enemy," I slowly began to see something else — a human being. A mother. A daughter. A wife. A sister. A friend. That day my learned narrative formed a huge crack — a crack that eventually became a canyon as I steadily unlearned everything I was taught to know.

Within a country and globally, people talk about unity as if it's something that can be achieved easily. Or we speak about it in such a romanticized way that it seems unattainable, like it is completely out of reach. Unity can only happen when we are willing to connect and when we are willing to believe that everyone on this planet deserves to be able to give their children what Fatima wanted for her children — enough. Enough naturally creates opportunities. Toward the end of Gandhi's life, he was deeply hurt by the way that Hindus and Muslims in India turned against one another, using hatred and violence to eventually create a partition of the country. One side would blame the other for all the ailments of society, pointing to the other religion as the cause of this angst. Had he lived, I wonder what Gandhi would have done to heal the communal divides that exist today — between not just Hindus and Muslims but also Christians, tribal peoples, and those deemed sub-human ("untouchable") by the caste system? I believe that he would have first gone to live among them, tending to the sick and serving the poor. I believe he would have asked his supporters and devotees to leave their own colonies and go serve in other colonies. He understood clearly that it was his duty "to love and serve [my neighbors]. How can there be a neighborhood without contact, and a community without neighborhood?" Doing this challenges the depths of alienation people experience and strips us of fear. It allows for the mask to fall off, the veil to be removed. It reminds us of the humanness of a local community of relationships.

Returning to the issue of equity, a move back to more local production and consumption would create an economy that de-centralizes political power. This doesn't mean trying to stop or re-wind globalization, but true democracy is practiced at the local level. This is how changes are made and movements are built — in small increments and in local areas. The most "local" place that exists is under your feet. Change and movement begin with you, and they require — as I have experienced — awakening from the trance of our assumptions. Here is a story that deeply mo-tivated me about the possibility that shifts can occur anywhere and that our hearts can crack open at any time. It was written by Nancy Dahlberg, a now-retired reverend and spiritual leader, and shared at a retreat I attended. Here is what Nancy wrote:

It's Sunday, Christmas. Our family has spent the holiday in San Francisco with my husband's parents, but to get back to work the next day, we had to drive the four hundred miles to Los Angeles on Christmas Day. We stopped for lunch in King City. And we walked into a diner. One of those where everybody was silent and everything was quiet, there wasn't much going on. I sat Eric, our one-year-old, in a high chair and looked around the room and wondered, what am I doing in this place? No sense of, really, the holidays. And my reverie was interrupted when I heard Eric squeal with glee.

"Hi there!"

Two words you thought were one. "Hi there!" He pounded his fat baby hands, whack, whack, on the metal high-chair tray. His face was alive with excitement, gums bared in a toothless grin. He wriggled and chirped and I saw the source of his merriment, and my eyes couldn't take it all in at once.

A tattered rag of a coat bought by someone obviously eons ago, both ends, zipper half-masked over his spindly body, toes that poked out of would-be shoes, a shirt that had ring around the collar all over it, and a face with gums as bare as Eric's, hair uncombed, whiskers too short to be called a beard, but way beyond a shadow. A nose so filled with varicose veins that it looked like a map of New York. I was too far away to smell him but I knew he smelled. And his hands were waving in the air, flapping on loose wrists.

"Hi there, baby! Hi there, big boy! I see you, buster!"

My husband and I exchanged a look that was a cross between "what do we do" and part devil.

Eric continued to engage, laugh, and answer "hiya!" Every call was echoed. I noticed waitresses' eyebrows shoot to their forehead. Several people "he-hemmed" out loud.

This old geezer was creating a nuisance with my beautiful baby.

I shoved a cracker at Eric, and he pulverized it on the tray. I whispered, "Why me?" under my breath. Our meal came, and the nuisance continued.

Next thing you know, the bum was shouting from across the room, "Do you know patty cake? Atta boy! You know peek-a-boo? Hey, look, he knows peek-a-boo."

Nobody thought it was cute.

That guy was probably a drunk. And definitely a disturbance. And I was embarrassed. My husband, Dennis, was humiliated. We ate in silence. Except Eric, who was running through his repertoire for his blaring applause from a skid-row bum.

Finally, I had enough. I turned the high chair. Eric screamed and clamored to face his old buddy. Now I was really mad.

Dennis went to pay the check and implored me to "get Eric and meet me in the parking lot." I trundled Eric out of the high chair and looked toward the exit. The only way out was past the man who sat poised and waiting, his chair directly between me and the door.

"Lord just let me out of here before he speaks to me or Eric."

I headed to the door.

It soon became apparent that both the Lord and Eric had other plans.

As I drew closer to the man, I turned my back, walking to sidestep him and any air he might be breathing, and as I did, Eric, all the while with eyes riveted to his best friend, leaned far over my arm, reaching with both arms out in a baby "pick me up" position.

In a split second, I went from balancing my baby to turning toward the counter for weight, and I came eye to eye with the old man. Eric was lunging for him. Arms spread wide.

The bum's eyes both asked and implored, "Would you let me hold your baby?"

There was no need for me to answer. Eric propelled himself from my arms into the man's. Suddenly, a very old man and a very young baby were involved in a loving relationship. Eric laid his tiny head on the man's ragged shoulder. The man's eyes closed, and I saw tears hover beneath his lashes. His aged hands full of grime and pain and hard labor gently, so gently cradled my baby's bottom and stroked his back.

I stood there awestruck. The man rocked and cradled Eric for a few moments, and then his eyes opened and set squarely on mine. He said in a firm, commanding voice, "You take care of this baby." Somehow I managed "I will" from a throat that contained a stone.

He pried Eric from his chest unwillingly, longingly, as though he wasn't ready to give him up. I held my arms open and ready to receive my baby, and again the gentleman addressed me. "God bless you, ma'am. You've given me my Christmas gift." I said nothing more than a muttered "thanks." With Eric back in my arms, I ran for the car. Dennis wondered why I was crying and holding Eric so tightly, and why I was saying, "My god, my god, forgive me, forgive me."

At the retreat, I remember listening to that being read as tears streamed down my face. I thought about all the people I saw through a narrow or foggy lens and wondered how many I had not slowed down enough to see at all. The only hope we have for unity and equity, for there to be no barriers to entry in our communities, is to connect to our common humanity, to feel and sense compassion, and to slow down enough to see who is there long enough to respond from a place steeped in love.

CHAPTER TWELVE

If Only for Today

There are only two days in the year that nothing can be done.
One is called yesterday, the other is called tomorrow,
so today is the right day to love, believe, do, and mostly live.

— DALAI LAMA

On a cool-for-Florida Saturday in March 2019, one day before the one-year anniversary of the global March for Our Lives protests, I was scheduled to teach a class down in Miami's South Beach — not a place you want to be driving to on a sunny Saturday during the height of snowbird season, when northerners fatigued by snowy cities are looking for any patch of sand and sunshine in which to land. Miami is an interesting place — the ever-changing zoning always seems to have one consistent characteristic. You can be driving through a neighborhood of million-dollar homes and instantly be surrounded by Section 8 housing, having entered a neighborhood you don't want to get lost in at night.

Earlier that week, I had morning coffee with my friend

Jason — to learn more about his business and how I could help open doors for him. Jason is married to my friend Samantha, a tiny but fierce speech pathologist from Parkland, Florida. Samantha took on a role that nobody would ever want — she became a lead chairperson for March for Our Lives after the devastating shooting at Marjory Stoneman Douglas High School in 2018. Samantha is an alumna of the high school, her mom is a teacher there who was at the school during the shooting, and Sam personally knew a lot of the families impacted by it.

In passing, Jason mentioned to me that he had heard about a hunger strike taking place in Liberty City, one of those dangerous, "Section 8" neighborhoods that visitors to Miami are told to avoid. The strikers, organized by a community organization called the Circle of Brotherhood, called themselves the "Hunger 9." They were trying to bring attention to the ongoing gun violence and loss of life in their predominantly Black neighborhood. When a Black teenager is hit by a stray bullet in Liberty City, the media doesn't really cover it because it's seen as "just another day." As someone who considers herself super plugged-in to both local and national news, it outraged me that I hadn't heard about the hunger strike sooner. Were the lives of young Black boys in "the hood" less important than the lives of white students in affluent suburbs like Parkland?

That Saturday morning, Samantha was driving down with me to attend my workshop, and I suggested that, once it was over, we could stop at the strike to show solidarity. Sam agreed, but she and I had no idea what to expect when we rolled up to the encampment of tents on an empty dirt lot at a busy intersection. At the gate, a heavy-set man sitting on a folding chair looked us up and down and asked us what we wanted. We explained that we were representing the Parkland community and wanted to show solidarity with the strikers. He said the strikers were resting. By then, it was the eleventh day of the hunger strike, so they needed to preserve their energy. The man said to come back in a few hours when "visiting hours" were in session. Sam and I looked at each other, disappointed, and turned to walk away, when suddenly we heard, "Hold on! Wait!" We turned around. A tall, thin, bald Black man in a Hunger 9 T-shirt waved us back. When we explained who we were, his eyes widened with excitement and he let us in. The man, who introduced himself affectionately as Brother Lyle, took us into the camp and explained the motivation behind this movement. He detailed how real the struggle is — pointing out the banner zip-tied to the chain-link fence listing the names of the hundreds of lives lost to gun violence in the last year, and then he walked us into the tents lined with cots and introduced us, one by one, to each of the brave members of the Hunger 9.

Brother Albert was lying on his cot. He managed to sit up and was about to stand when I kneeled beside him and put my hand on top of his hand. "We're Shelly and Samantha, and we drove down to represent the Parkland community," I explained. Albert said nothing. We spent a few long minutes just gazing directly into each other's eyes, with tears streaming down our cheeks. When Albert broke the silence, he told us in a soft-spoken voice and deliberate delivery how he had been incarcerated for thirty-five years. He admitted that he was one of the brothers in the group who had done some things in his community that kept him up at night. "I never killed anyone," he said, but he quickly added that he didn't know if the drugs that he sold on the streets before he was arrested had led to somebody's death. He admitted that he believes his generation left an inheritance of bloodshed and murder for the current generation. While he was in prison, he promised God that, if he was ever let out, he would come back to his community and do all that he could to undo the damage. In 2016, Albert was released because of the clemency project initiated by President Barack Obama.

This is a story about what happens when we show up for one another. It's a story about what happens when we stop questioning our differences and wondering *if* people will accept us. Most importantly, it's a story about what happens *after* we show up — will we decide to continue showing up and to stick around? Are we committed for the long term, or do we just show up for the photo opportunity? This is a story about what can happen when we utter four little words: "What do you need?" or "How can I help?" These words can open up a portal, a door to the heart, to opportunity. If we take a moment to ask and then truly listen, we can receive a road map to enact change. On that day, I looked Albert in the eyes and promised him that I would never forget him, that I would never let him down intentionally, and that I would do whatever I could to bring resources to his community. As Albert and I hugged goodbye that day, I said: "Dear Brother, I will never abandon you."

Ever since and to this day, I've been working hand in hand with Brother Lyle and the Circle of Brotherhood to bring trauma-informed healing practices to the community in and around Liberty City. We amplify their stories where we can, and we also bring in strategic partners so they can continue to do amazing things and create shifts within their community. This is a story of what happens when people recognize their wealth and their privilege and what they can do for others, and then connect using the language of the heart and, in this case, the language of loss. I've learned through my work that these languages are the same the whole world over. The question is: Are you willing to speak those languages and then move to action in places that make you feel uncomfortable but that need you the most?

If you had asked me that question a decade earlier, my answer would likely have been no. I was not then always willing to move outside my comfort zone. I wasn't unwilling to be uncomfortable, but in some situations, I didn't always believe my actions would make a difference. I would get stuck at a familiar crossroads — feeling overwhelmed, unable to make a decision, and suffering analysis paralysis. I would say things like, "What's the point of showing up?" or "What can one person do? Nothing I do is going to matter." To move beyond ourselves — our own universe — to tend to our communities, and then to have the capacity and will to extend ourselves to other communities, we need to resolve that we will no longer live our lives centered around goals, but centered around intention. There is a huge difference. Focusing on intention means living a heart-centered life. It means that, regardless of the outcome, we try to consistently act in alignment with our true self, our true purpose ... our truth.

Focus on Who You Want to Be, Not What You Achieve

When we are young, adults always ask us, "What do you want to be when you grow up?" That is a goal-oriented question, and it leads to a goal-oriented response. It makes *what* we are seem most important — whether that's a cowboy, princess, doctor, or lawyer — and I think this question should be retired. I think it leads to the stifled, self-defeating fears that keep us, as adults, from showing up. Instead, we should ask ourselves: *Who* do we want to be? That is, what kind of person? Someone who is compassionate, helpful, loving? This question elicits a response that focuses on our intentions. Rather than focus on what we might achieve in any material way, or what title or profession we might pursue, we consider how we want to show up every single day of our lives in everything we do. Living our life centered around intentions informs *every* area of our life.

It can be easy to confuse intentions with goals, since sometimes we use the same language for both. For instance, someone could say, "My intention is to be happy," but this turns happiness into a goal or something to achieve. As we all know, wanting to be happy does not by itself make us happier. If anything, this can leave us even more frustrated, since many days we may not achieve or feel happiness, no matter how hard we try. However, instead, if we say, "My intention is to act with kindness," then what matters is how we act, our effort, not the result. Further, we always have the power to choose how to act, and we can be kind in any circumstance, even in the most mundane aspects of our lives. And if we do this each day, little by little, that intention to be kind will become part of the fabric of who we are.

Here is how I try to do this in my own life, using an exercise I learned and adapted from the meditation teacher and author Lodro Rinzler. Every morning when I wake up, sometimes before I even open my eyes, I ask myself the same question: "What intention do I want to cultivate more of in my life today?" Then I answer the question with a single word. For a few moments, I consider: If I were able to completely embody a specific intention all day, what word would most significantly create a shift for me, for those in my community, and the world around me? Some days the word arrives instantly; sometimes it is the same word day after day for a stretch of several weeks. Sometimes I have to really dig deep to even have a single word arise. Words that have popped up for me again and again include patience, compassion, self-care, self-love, and joy.

Then I get out of bed, shuffle over to the bathroom for my morning routine, and after staring into the mirror (sometimes frightening myself by what is staring back at me), I grab a dry-erase marker — the kind used on whiteboards that can be erased with a swipe of your hand — and write on the mirror the one word that came to me that morning. That word becomes my intention for the day. I look myself square in the eyes and say to myself, "*If only for today*, I am going to infuse more [intention word] in every area of my life. If only for today." Then I carry on with my day — attending meetings, making calls, writing and exercising, making dinner, running errands, walking the dog and picking up dog poop, washing the dishes, and folding laundry.

On some days I remember my intention word throughout my day. For example, let's say my word is *kindness*, and that day, a client named Judith keeps calling me and being needy and indecisive. In order to decide how to respond, I would ask myself: *If only for today, if I were to treat Judith with more kindness, what would that look like?* My answer might be this: *If only for today, in order to treat Judith with more kindness, every time she calls, whether it is the second, fourth, or seventh time, I will act like it is the first time she has called me today.* The key phrase is "if only for today." Tomorrow is another day. Tomorrow, I might have a different intention word. Tomorrow, I may lose my patience with Judith ... but *if only for today*, I will try to infuse kindness in every interaction I have. This includes interactions with myself. If that day I also go to yoga class, rather than looking around at the human contortionists folding themselves into pretzels while I can barely touch my toes, I would say to myself: *If only for today, I will treat myself with more kindness and not compare myself to others. I will give myself props for showing up and administering self-care.* Here again, the key phrase is "if only for today." Tomorrow is another day. Tomorrow, I might beat myself up for not getting to yoga class, or I might get frustrated with myself that after over a decade of practicing yoga, I still can't do a headstand. But at least for that day, I will try and infuse kindness into every part of my day.

At the end of the day, I return to the bathroom for my night-time routine, and while staring at my reflection in the mirror, I consider the word written on the mirror in dry-erase marker. As I brush my teeth, I go through the entire day's activities, frame by frame — click, click, click — as if my brain is clicking through a View-Master slideshow. In each instance, I think: *Was I kind when I did this activity or that one? Was I kind when I interacted with this person? Was I kind to myself?* Sometimes, the answer is a resounding *yes!* If so, I take a moment, after spitting and rinsing of course, to pat myself on the back. I celebrate my little victory and think, *Wow! I was kind today!*

Sometimes, however, when I replay the day's moments and interactions, I am not particularly impressed with my achievements. There are even some days when I am so distracted or in a fog that I forget about the intention word completely until I see it on the mirror in the evening. Whatever the case, whether I am celebrating or disappointed, I remind myself: *It is only for today.* Before turning off the lights and heading to bed, I wipe away the word with the palm of my hand because tomorrow is another day. Tomorrow, there will be another word or maybe it will be the same word. Either way, I will be presented with a new opportunity to center every activity and interaction in my life around my intention.

On the day I met Brother Albert at the Hunger 9 encampment, my word was *presence*. I think that subconsciously that word popped into my brain that morning because I was going to teach a two-and-a-half-hour workshop that would require me to be fully present while teaching, but also afterward when speaking to students as they detailed their experiences, concerns, and needs. Sometimes, after teaching, it isn't always easy to stay fully present and hold the space for others, but I was determined to infuse that intention into my day. Presence, both physically and mentally, anchored me that day, kneeling at Brother Albert's feet, standing at the gate of the encampment with Samantha, listening and taking in the stories of the brave men and the pain and strife in their community.

The problems of the world are daunting, I know. They seem enormous, too big for any single person to carry, really. Most days, it is easier to walk away from global problems and crises, since on most days we are facing our own issues and have our own reckonings to contend with. If we have a community of care or if we are engaged in mutual aid, we may already feel overburdened. Yet I believe, if we make it our intention, we can always do more — in each moment, in each day, in each interaction … *even if only for today*. When we center our actions around an intention, day after day, then we can find ways to tackle communal or global problems in individual ways. Large problems become easier to bear, to hold. We can feel like we are chipping away, making a dent, creating a ripple, planting a seed. Simply by being present for others, by being kind to someone who is struggling, or by being patient with those who disagree or hold opposing views. In every single instance, in incremental ways, we can create a shift — even including with social justice, equity, and peace — with *our contribution*, which is the only thing in our control. Instead of feeling small, we can feel empowered, knowing that whatever we do — the action, the word, the gesture, the look, the hug, the presence — is, in fact, a singular pebble being thrown into the pond that generates a ripple that may reach shores far beyond our comprehension. In our lifetime, we can throw many pebbles. *If only for today*, we can commit to throwing at least one.

Getting Back More Than We Give

Many summers ago, I went down to city hall to pay for a parking ticket in person because I could not take care of it online. As I stood in line waiting for the next clerk, I overheard a frazzled woman explain to a man behind the counter why she didn't pay her parking ticket on time and had incurred the late fees. She was making a case to try and get him to waive the penalty, which nearly doubled the cost of the ticket.

She said, "Most days, I am late to pick up my son from daycare because my boss has me running his personal errands after hours. I parked in a metered spot outside of the daycare for just a moment as I ran in, and when I came out, my car had a ticket. I was there for five minutes. I am sure that was even caught on a surveillance camera somewhere. I can barely afford the late fees at daycare. This is going to cripple me." She paused and then continued, "I agreed to take on these extra tasks so that I don't lose my job. I can't be picky in this economy. I'm a single mom."

I really felt for this woman. I understood where she was coming from and understood her struggle on a personal level. Because

I connected with her story, I wanted to do something to let her know she was not alone. At the time, I could not afford to pay her ticket for her — things were tight for me as well. What could I offer her?

My desire to spontaneously give something to her, to help her not feel alone, was instinctive. I felt it was my duty to pay things forward because of all the help I had gotten when I was not in a position to give anything to anyone. I remembered that, at a school bingo night, I had won a gift certificate to a popular, local ice cream shop. While my son was proud of that "win," would he know the difference, I reasoned, if I just paid for his next cone? Unsuccessful with her plea, the woman paid her ticket and the penalty and walked away looking defeated. I abandoned my place in line and followed her out of the building, calling out to her while waiving the gift certificate in my hand.

"Excuse me! I'm so sorry," I said. "I know this is strange, and maybe even a bit creepy, but I couldn't help overhear your conversation with the clerk in there. I'm sorry it didn't work out the way you wanted it to, but I wanted you to know that I think you are doing an amazing job as a parent, and I want you to feel seen." I handed her the certificate and said, "Take your son for an ice cream or two. Just enjoy each other and the moment."

Her eyes welled up with tears, and she managed to say, "Thank you." She opened her arms and gave me a heartfelt hug. What I offered this woman was not a scoop of butter pecan, but a small gesture of solidarity and understanding.

In 2015, PBS aired a three-part series called *This Emotional Life*, exploring the healing power of giving through volunteerism and philanthropy. Research shows that once people have enough to meet their needs, additional money and time do not increase their happiness. It's only when the donor gives away the additional money and time that the donor's happiness is increased. People benefit the most by connecting with others in a tangible way that makes both the giver and receiver realize that they are not alone. It doesn't matter what type of giving we are talking about. It can be words of encouragement, a gift certificate to an ice cream shop, or a large-scale operation like Habitat for Humanity, where people are working together to build a home for a family that does not have one. What matters the most is not how much is given, but how it is given.

This is what it means to speak the language of the heart. If we give compassionately with a desire to connect, it is much more satisfying than if we give out of obligation or because we want to inflate our self-esteem. *If only for today*, pay closer attention to every person you encounter — people you know, acquaintances, and even perfect strangers. Ask: What intention do I want to embody? Start there and see how quickly seemingly small acts of kindness and connection ripple out.

CHAPTER THIRTEEN

Creating Sustainable Movements

Trust only movements. Life happens at the level of events,
not words. Trust movement.

— ALFRED ADLER

Movements are not goals. There are no finish lines. There are only incremental gains that require consistent forward motion born out of actionable intentions. Creating sustainable movements requires widening our perspective of self-care, shifting it from a purely individual pursuit to one that embraces the entire community and uses the entire toolbox of best practices and resources. While self-care and communal care are movements in themselves, they also provide the primary infrastructure that supports every other movement — whether for equity, justice, peace, or freedom. Movements are a marathon, not a sprint, and in order to sustain forward movement — even if it's millimeter by painful millimeter at a time — the pillar of societal care must be championed. Take a moment to imagine the power of a self-care movement — a wave of kind care connecting communities, healing our bodies and minds, sustaining our energy and momentum, and helping us all live healthier, happier, and more balanced lives. That's pretty awesome.

This is not new. As a movement, self-care has a rich and even radical history. It was born at the intersection of the women's liberation movement and the civil rights era, a time when brave individuals were fighting the relentless enemies of prejudice and discrimination. These American heroes created the first formalized communities of care, which allowed them to stand strong together in the face of seemingly impossible challenges and unspeakable treatment. In fact, what they were fighting for was — and remains — the basic human right to self-care. People of color were often denied medical treatment at hospitals and health care centers. The government had turned its back on them, and so self-care, quite literally, became a matter of life and death; part of what they were fighting for was the freedom, time, money, and resources to care for themselves. In this exhausting battle, often the only support they found was with one another and within themselves. What was true for the civil rights movement was also true for the women's liberation movement. Women and people of color viewed controlling their health as a corrective to the failures of a white, patriarchal medical system to properly tend to their needs. Self-care, as described by Natalia Mehlman Petrzela, an assistant professor at the New School in New York City, became "a claiming [of] autonomy over the body as a political act against institutional, technocratic, very racist, and sexist medicine." Civil rights leaders made health care a priority. As Martin Luther King Jr. said, "Of all the forms of inequality, injustice in health is the most shocking and the most inhuman."

In this age of the industrial wellness complex, in an era of bath bombs, drop-in meditation studios, and face masks, it's easy to forget that, for marginalized populations, self-care is neither frivolous nor easy. As a movement, self-care and communal care make the bold, inspiring declaration that *we don't just deserve to be alive; we have the right to live our best lives*. Seen this way, self-care isn't superficial; it isn't a self-help list of quick tips to feel better or avoid the undesirable. Genuine self-care and communal care are long and hard. They require diving beneath the surface problems, which are just the symptoms of the deeper, more enduring trauma that all of us carry. What we need, and what this movement seeks, is — to use a concept coined by Ghanaian playwright and journalist Esther Armah — emotional justice.

Emotional justice can provide us with a steady undercurrent, like a river flowing beneath the hard exterior crust of the Earth's mantle, as we embark on dismantling and rebuilding social systems that don't work for us. Emotional justice depends upon our commitment to doing the inner work; it cannot exist without it. This type of work can show up in different forms, like healing from an offense that was never recognized by the offender or by society or having the courage to speak up for ourselves and write our own stories. "Feel-good" moments will not sustain us and allow us to go the distance that the marathon of movements requires. In social and political movements, commitment to community care, which means our own — and others' — emotional justice is a fundamental building block.

Doing the inner work in order to feel good about ourselves is not enough to support a movement. We cannot only turn inward for our own benefit. What defines any movement — including the self-care movement — is people coming together with a shared purpose to create change that benefits everyone. Of course, successful movements require strong leadership and partnerships, support from stakeholders, well-defined goals, and a solid plan, but more than anything else, they require passionate members. They need people with skin in the game and the energy and desire to move the needle and drive change.

In recent years, a growing uneasiness and an undercurrent of anxiety have emerged in America — regardless of what side of the political spectrum people are on. Psychologists, therapists, social workers, and doctors alike agree that we are in the middle of a genuine national mental health crisis. However, times like these can serve as the impetus for a self-care movement that can have a profound and lasting impact on this country. We have the opportunity to reclaim the term *self-care* so that, as the late activist Audre Lorde said, it's not considered "self-indulgent" but an act of "self-preservation." For self-care to become a national movement, we must clearly define what self-care is and what it's for: its intention and purpose. The point isn't to achieve a particular "goal." As a movement, it's not about realizing our own in-the-moment happiness. Rather, it's seeing that our self-care impacts the lives of those around us in innumerable positive ways. Self-care reaches beyond the individual to impact communities, neighborhoods, our nation, and ultimately, the world.

Bringing Positive Change to the Collective Struggle

Building a self-care movement — one that can support every other movement in turn — requires incorporating it into our communities and workplaces so that "communities of care" become part of our culture. Some approaches to this are easy, while others are more complex, but they are all areas that need to be explored. First, we must eradicate the stigmatization of mental health. In fact, those who create communities of care where they live become de facto leaders in this. In their own ways, they bring positive energy and workable solutions to those struggling with mental health issues, which helps change the way we look at mental health in this country. Ultimately, we want to make sure every person has access to the caregivers, transportation, treatment, and funds needed to properly address mental health.

We all need to commit to sharing our self-care knowledge with one another. We each have daily routines and personal challenges, but we don't have to go it alone. When we take the time to create space in our schedules for others, when we organize and meet up with friends and social groups, and even when we exchange thoughtful emails, we're building communities of care and, therefore, fueling the self-care revolution — one person at a time. The way we set the positive intentions for groups makes a difference and helps create guilt-free, inviting spaces where all individuals in our networks can enjoy the added support of a caring community.

Each of us can help define the standards. The slow adoption of self-care in our culture is in big part due to a lack of definition. People don't know what the standards of self-care are or should be because these have never been clearly established. So one mission is to create a well-defined vision for self-care grounded in real principles and standards. When I was the president of a large service company, when a client would complain about customer service, I would first examine whether or not we, as a company, properly defined the expectations for the client. I couldn't expect my team to meet or exceed the expectations if they weren't clearly defined. I couldn't hold people accountable if they fell short unless expectations had been formalized. The same is true here. By defining the standards for self-care, we legitimize our cause by providing a clear road map for people to follow. Then people can create plans, measure progress, and make changes based on realistic and achievable goals. I define self-care as the practice of taking an active role in protecting our own well-being, pursuing happiness, and having the ability, tools, and resources to respond to periods of stress so that they don't result in imbalance and lead to a health crisis.

Further, we need to remember that exhausted leadership is poor leadership. The reward for productivity should not be the assignment of more work — whether for ourselves, a paid employee, or a volunteer. Exhaustion leads to shorter attention spans, increased emotional volatility, and poor decision making. No matter what our role or involvement, we help create a sustainable self-care movement by modeling sustainable self-care in our lives and workplaces. If we burn out, that will be replicated by others in our sphere of influence — coworkers, staff, volunteers, children, and so on. Social transformation work begins with the self. When we imagine what advocacy work looks like visually, for example, perhaps we can see it as a series of peaks and valleys. The peaks are where advocacy work happens, and the valleys are where we rest, celebrate, and reflect, gathering our strength to climb the mountain ahead. If we conduct our lives this way and model this workflow in our organizations, we can build resilience, make sure that we keep people engaged, and ensure that none of us fall victim to burnout.

We need to constantly, at every turn and with every incremental step forward, ask ourselves and those on our teams and in our communities reflective questions that can improve our actions and build momentum to climb the next peak. Key questions that will help us improve self-care habits include the following:

- How does the quality of my leadership diminish due to the lack of my own self-care?
- Which habits negatively impact my self-care, and what new behavior can I substitute for them?
- Do I have a self-care plan in place to ensure I follow up on new behaviors, and have I shared this plan with others who will hold me accountable?
- How will I track my progress along the way?
- How can I best support others in their endeavors?

The modern self-care movement can embody practices that avoid burnout, rather than merely be a response to it. The movement must demand that individuals put their health and wellness first without feeling guilty for doing so. If we all collectively share our plans for self-care, we declare boldly that *our needs, our state of mind, our body, and our overall health matter.* This gives others permission to invest in themselves and take the courageous step to acknowledge that they have needs, that their needs are important, and that those needs deserve to be met.

This is a plea to integrate self-care with community care and social movements, paving the path forward to achieve balance between all three and to cease having to choose one over the other. When we work on the self, we do not need to abandon the world. Connecting personal self-care with communal care that benefits the world is a lifelong pursuit. Working on the self is a task that will never be finished, not until the day we expire. We need to commit to this work for the rest of our lives, constantly striving to improve, hone, and refine. When we begin this process with ourselves, we begin the journey of working to heal our community and the world.

In Sanskrit, the term for self-actualization and individuation is *samadhi*, which means enlightenment or union with the divine. This word recognizes that we are more than just our individual selves; we are a sum of all the parts that surround us. Each human life is valued, and we are all connected, and when we recognize this, we can embark on the healing work that addresses the traumas of our culture. By starting with the inner work, we address many of our root issues and work our way through them.

Today, we are seeing calls for change and transformation of our world. We are seeing people rise up in their power to assert that their lives are important, valuable, and worth fighting for. We are also showing solidarity by giving our friends and loved ones messages of strength and support as they dismantle systems that are oppressive and archaic. If we all simultaneously commit to healing ourselves and healing our trauma, our own healing becomes a contribution to the community's health and wellness, to our descendants' health and wellness, and to the world's health and wellness.

It is my hope that we each show up, fractured or whole but always beautiful, with our unique talents and skills to create the world we envision for our children. Please remember that no action is too small, no voice is too quiet, and no person is too insignificant to make a change. May you realize that your investment in the inner work awakens awareness to something else, something quite radical and liberating, a possibility. You matter, your voice matters, your life is precious, and you have so many gifts to offer. When our inner work is deeply embodied in the collective life of those working for social transformation, this creates resilience within the group, so that when natural bumps or boulders in the journey arise, we don't give up. Instead, we stay the course, adjust course, or shore up our reserves and capacity. We celebrate and introduce play, creativity, and lightness into our efforts. We remember the purpose, meaning, and inspiration behind what we're doing, and it buoys us to keep going.

My eldest uncle, a very pious man, would always share with me wisdom from the Old Testament and the Talmud (also known as the Oral Torah). One of the verses that he shared with me from the Talmud when I was barely thirteen has been a guidepost for my work: "Do not be daunted by the enormity of the world's grief. Do justly now, love mercy now, walk humbly now. You are not obligated to complete the work, but neither are you free to abandon it."

I only know this: Our purpose is to love, and that means that we must show up so that our work can allow love to be continuously released into the world. We are not free to abandon that work, lest we intend to abandon the world and, in turn, ourselves. The suffering on this planet is just an outward reflection of our inner suffering — an accumulation of billions of human beings who are not taking responsibility for their internal strife. If we each only make a commitment not to abandon ourselves, we've successfully cast a pebble in the pond. The ripple is guaranteed.

Afterword

To read this book is to take a journey. We step into discovery and adventure, our hand enfolded in Shelly's. She lovingly reassures us that she doesn't hesitate to insist on our own progress. "You have to show up" is her assertion to us from beginning to end. Shelly clearly understands the courage showing up may take — the heartfulness and the audacity and the letting go of habit it often does take — yet she never pulls back from what she knows to be true: "You have to show up."

It's not easy to write in a way that is both deeply personal and universally applicable as you explore topics of suffering, loss, identity. Even topics like joy and self-care, community and generosity might serve to remind people more of what they feel they don't have than of what they can in truth access in this very moment. Shelly's book strikes the perfect balance between the personal and the universal. Even as we experience awe at the tenacity, vision, and caring manifested in her journey, we don't feel at all diminished by witnessing that journey; instead, we feel vastly empowered by it.

That's what makes this book both visionary and practical. As just one example, who among us has not felt overwhelmed by the changing circumstances of life? (Maybe we do right now, in fact.) In those times, the reminder to take things in chunks instead of trying to deal with everything all at once seems way too simple, and yet is madly useful. Implicit in that reminder is the reinforcement of our sense of agency, forgiveness for whatever we are feeling, the recognition that our ability to be aware is much more powerful than whatever we may be aware of in any moment, and a great deal more.

Through the years I've known Shelly, this is how I've come to understand what makes her special: When something bad happens in the world, I find myself gradually taking in the suffering, over time coming to acknowledge it more fully, slowly thinking of how I might respond to help bring some relief to those in pain. In the meantime, Shelly has immediately seen the need, mapped out a plan, and already put the pieces and people together to implement it. She has the energy of at least a hundred people. Now that I'm older, the word *effective* has a whole new allure for me. It is a trait I admire a lot. In *Sit Down to Rise Up* the keys to Shelly's extraordinary effectiveness are laid out for each of us to consider.

In that light, Shelly often points to the questions she recommends we ask ourselves, rather than providing predetermined answers we somehow are obliged to arrive at. Through encouraging meditations, reflections, and journaling, Shelly provides a path to genuine change in our lives via the development of self-awareness and self-compassion. She herself has already lived several lifetimes within this one, and in the book reveals both the highs and the lows she has been through. Because of her honesty and courage, we can find ourselves in her life even if the specific circumstances of our own are completely different. That's why, in reading this book, we feel we have found a dear friend in Shelly, and no matter what our own life looks like, we see we are not walking this path to freedom alone.

— SHARON SALZBERG, author of *Lovingkindness*
and *Real Happiness*, cofounder of the
Insight Meditation Society in Barre, Massachusetts

Sources

Chapter 1: Agency

Côté, J. E. "The Role of Identity Capital in the Transition to Adulthood: The Individualization Thesis Examined." *Journal of Youth Studies* 5, no. 2 (2002): 117–34.

Côté, J. E., and J. M. Bynner. "Changes in the Transition to Adulthood in the UK and Canada: The Role of Structure and Agency in Emerging Adulthood." *Journal of Youth Studies* 11 (2008): 251–68.

Côté, J. E., and C. G. Levine. *Identity Formation, Agency, and Culture: A Social Psychological Synthesis*. Mahwah, NJ: Lawrence Erlbaum Associates Publishers, 2002.

Frankl, Viktor E. *Man's Search for Meaning: An Introduction to Logotherapy*. New York: Simon & Schuster, 1984. Quote: page 137.

Chapter 4: Familiarization

Fujita, K., et al. "Construal Levels and Self-Control." *Journal of Personality and Social Psychology* 90, no. 3 (2006): 351–67. https://doi.org/10.1037/0022-3514.90.3.351.

Job, Veronika, et al. "Ego Depletion — Is It All in Your Head? Implicit Theories about Willpower Affect Self-Regulation." *Psychological Science* 21, no. 11 (November 2010): 1686–93. doi:10.1177/0956797610384745.

Chapter 6: Kindsight

"Black Box." *Radiolab*, NPR/WNYC Studios, January 17, 2014. https://www
.globalplayer.com/podcasts/episodes/3yycg1.
James, William. *The Varieties of Religious Experience*. London: Penguin
Books, 1982. Quote: page 157.

Chapter 9: Circles of Influence and the Ripple Effect

Cialdini, Robert. *Pre-Suasion: A Revolutionary Way to Influence and Per-
suade*. New York: Simon & Schuster, 2016.
Covey, Stephen B. *The Seven Habits of Highly Effective People*. New York:
Free Press, 1989/2004. Quote: pages 82–83.
Niemiec, Ryan M. *Mindfulness and Character Strengths: A Practical Guide
to Flourishing*. Boston: Hogrefe Publishing, 2014.

Chapter 10: Mutual Aid: Solidarity, Not Charity

"Catholic Health Care during the Coronavirus Pandemic." *Jesuitical*
(podcast) in *America: The Jesuit Review*, March 20, 2020. https://www
.americamagazine.org/politics-society/2020/03/20/podcast-catholic
-health-care-during-coronavirus-pandemic.
Padamsee, Yashna. "Communities of Care, Organizations for Liberation."
Naya maya (blog), June 19, 2011. https://nayamaya.wordpress.com.
Schneider, Nathan. "How to Build Mutual Aid That Will Last after the
Coronavirus Pandemic." *America: The Jesuit Review*, April 1, 2020.
https://www.americamagazine.org/politics-society/2020/04/01/how
-build-mutual-aid-will-last-after-coronavirus-pandemic.
Solnit, Rebecca. *A Paradise Built in Hell: The Extraordinary Communities
That Arise in Disaster*. New York: Penguin Random House, 2009.

Chapter 11: Enough Is a Feast

Bondurant, Joan. *Conquest of Violence: The Gandhian Philosophy of Conflict*. Princeton, NJ: Princeton University Press, 1988. Quote: page 155.

Acknowledgments

So many people have had (and will continue to have) a hand in shaping who I am and enriching my life. I did the best I could to remember to acknowledge each and every one of you; please forgive me if I did not mention you by name — there are so many people who have deeply imprinted on my heart over many lifetimes. You give me hope, you make me a better person, and you move me to act on behalf of all of us.

First, I want to thank the two most important people in my life — my biggest cheerleaders and loves of my life: my husband, Jason, and my son, Liam. You are both unwavering in your support of my dreams and your belief that I can manage to accomplish them. Jason, you have sacrificed so much to help me get to this point, and I could not have ever gotten to this moment without you by my side. I have wings because of you. I will love you until my final breath.

Liam, you were too young to know it then, but now you can read all about it: You saved me. I am a better human because you are my son. Thank you for sharing me with this project for so long and for always knowing when to say, "You got this."

Mom, the book is dedicated to you and rightly so. The strength and courage you have given to everything that you have had to face in your life — knowingly and unknowingly — have been passed on to me. You invested so much of your time, energy, and belief in me, and because of you, I am.

Dad, your talent with music, weaving words, and painting scenes and your affinity for languages were passed on to me. You more than provided for us; you made sure we didn't want for anything but that we also got more than we needed or even deserved. This access to experiences opened my eyes to the possibilities the world can offer up to those willing to seize them.

My older brothers, Izic and Omri, have always been heroes to me. Izic, your courage and vision in life have helped me realize that getting out of the rat race is possible and that I can live life on my own terms and start again. Omri, it's so hard to think of a childhood memory or a seminal moment from my formative years that doesn't include your influence or mentorship. You taught me to read and write — these words belong to you.

My sisters-in-law, Laura and Anne-Laure, who put up with me in the darker years, the lost years, and the selfish years: I admire both of you as individuals, as women, and as mothers, and I cherish you as my friends. My nieces and nephews — Shabtai, Caoba, Noam, and Velzy — you make life full.

My father-in-law, Zenon "Chuck" Tygielski, who I always half-jokingly say is "the reason why I married Jason": My love and admiration for him is infinite, and his excitement and support have meant the world to me.

My mother-in-law, Rowena Ryan Tygielski, is like my soul

sister. She keeps me grounded in optimism, wonder, and curiosity and is a reminder that pure love is possible. My Larry-in-Law keeps me inquisitive, fired up, and always yearning for truth.

Thank you to my Tygielski Crew — my brothers-in-law, David and Matthew, and my sisters-in-law, Jenny and Lisa. You make life fun, and you make it easy to have family.

To my entire clan throughout Israel — the Barashi, Biri, and Sitton families — who raised me, housed me, and gave me a free and beautiful childhood where I felt safe, and who, during my adolescence and adulthood, provided me with the foundation for the insights I have today.

My core teachers who have inspired and informed my work and without whom I would not have embarked on this journey or sustained it: my "Dipa Ma," Sharon Salzberg, and Jon Kabat-Zinn. Sharon, it was your prodding and encouragement that planted the seed. Your generosity in making introductions and opening doors means everything. You have my heart.

My University of Miami family — Scott Rogers and Dr. Amishi Jha.

This book (literally) would not have happened without the following people:

Anne Alexander, for planting the seed and telling me back in 2018 that I had a book inside of me waiting to come out.

Heather Hurlock, who bore witness and helped me write my first series ever for *Mindful* magazine and made me feel like a "real writer."

Lisa Weinert, who helped me birth the book proposal and coached me not just in writing but on life. I am so proud to call you a friend.

Jesseca Salky (and the entire Salky Literary Management

team), who is my "Jerry Maguire" — an agent who goes above and beyond and leads from her heart.

The entire team at New World Library — especially my fabulous editor, Jason Gardner ("the other Jason in my life"), and my unbelievable copy editor, Jeff Campbell — thank you for believing in this project and for helping to make it a reality.

Ina Lee, for your mentorship and encouragement, your ability to help keep me on course and to remind me about what I was put here on Earth to do: serve.

Paul Silitsky and Andrea Lubell, for helping to make sure I had the support I needed to get the proposal finished and the writing coach to get me to a manuscript.

Rachel Sapoznik, who provided me with a safety net and was the Thelma to my Louise when I took the leap and left my job in the corporate world and never looked back.

Gilda Ellison, who has always been in my village and is a long-lost sister. She is the one phone call I would make (and have made) if I needed someone to show up for me. I love you and I appreciate your presence in my life (and your family's presence).

Eliza Egan Smith and Grant Smith — and their children, Madeleine and Julian: Eliza for being part of the "original twelve" members of the sand tribe, who without hesitation has always shown up and gone above and beyond for me, even when I couldn't return the favor. You are a true friend, and I am lucky to have you in my corner. Grant, for your friendship and legal analysis whenever I needed it, and for letting me "borrow" Eliza whenever I needed her.

Miro Morfa and Steve Bullock. Miro, you are more than just my "emotional support person" but the best person I could have ever wished to have by my side on this journey.

My friend and soul brother davidji, who said "yes" to me and believed in the vision and makes the journey fun and meaningful.

The Pearson family in Glasgow, Scotland (Laura, Gavin, Max, Gabby, and Claudia) — and most especially to Laura, my forever roommate and the woman who will always be my "plus one."

The original twelve sand tribe members who showed up on that Sunday in November 2015, who started the momentum and kept showing up and bringing others; so much love for every single person who ever showed up on a Sunday morning in the last five years. Your showing up for me (and for yourselves) actually helped me show up for myself.

Chelsea and Simone Handler — your love and support have been such a wellspring of encouragement, and you have given me so much belief in myself. You are the sisters I have always wanted and finally was gifted with.

The entire Marjory Stoneman Douglas High School community, the cities of Parkland, Coral Springs, and Coconut Creek — and the "17 + 2" families who have given me the courage to speak up, show up, and *be* love, and most especially to:

The Dworets: Your friendship is one of the most meaningful ones I have ever had in my life; thank you for sharing Nick with all of us and allowing him to live on in each act of kindness and courage.

The Guttenbergs, for your open hearts and tireless efforts to make sure that the world is a better place for us all; thank you for sharing Jaime with us and for allowing us to honor her legacy each day. Fred, I am especially grateful for our connection and for modeling the way we can always show up for others.

The Schacters, for your bravery, your work across all divides, and your friendship; thank you for sharing Alex with us and for ensuring that he lives on through music.

The Alhadeffs, for the pure love you put into the universe, for always doing what is right and what is just, for reminding me to keep the faith and to remain hopeful; thank you for sharing Alyssa with us so that we can remember how to show up as leaders who lead with our heart.

Ivy Schamis and Prince Phillip — you will always be Mrs. Schamis to me, and I am so grateful for your guidance, mentorship, and purity of heart. You have touched so many lives throughout your career and have shaped so many minds and hearts — including my own.

Samantha and Jason Novick, whose presence has brought clarity, light, and motivation into my life; I love you both dearly.

My Purpose Over Pain family in Chicago — and most especially my sisters Brenda Mitchell, Anthanette Marshbanks, Pamela Bosely, Vera Smith, Elizabeth Bolden, Sharon Hatchett, and Diana Esco.

The entire Tree of Life Congregation in Pittsburgh, Pennsylvania — you keep me grounded in faith and show me what is possible from that space of trust.

The Circle of Brotherhood and the Hunger 9, and most especially to Brother Lyle, Brother Albert, and Brother Anthony.

The teachers who believed in me, invested in me, and saw something in me even when I didn't see it in myself: Mrs. Eleanor Morris, Mrs. Phyllis Pompeo-Phelps, Mrs. Sheryl Zigler, and Mrs. Gail Lowenstein Pachecho.

And I would be remiss not to mention the following:

- Sheila Garrick, Barbara Burggraaff, and Rhonda Magee, who made it okay to be "me" when I was stuck in a cycle of self-doubt and empowered me in a way that is still felt in my heart today

- The original "Brat Pack" — my community of care who loved and tended to me in my darkest days
- John and Jenny Zalkin
- Rodica and Charles Charles
- Meredith and Frank Domurat
- Susan Slate and Captain Sanderson
- Sandy and Lonnie Philips
- Jim Gimian
- Beth and Mark Eiglarsh
- Justin Michael Williams
- Dr. Dan Siegel and my MWe Family
- Soren Gordenhamer
- David Simas
- The cast and crew of Broward Meditates and HEAT Nation Meditation
- Shaul and Lilly Zislin
- Susanna Weiss and Allan Lokos
- Lisa Peddy
- The entire Strategic Forum family in South Florida
- Every single volunteer and chapter leader who showed up for Pandemic of Love
- Every Pandemic of Love donor
- Every Pandemic of Love recipient family
- Every amplifier who helped make the movement viral
- Every mentor and friend who has shown up for the movement and for me, including:
  - Sandy Grushow
  - Corey McGuire
  - Xander Shulz
  - Andrew Yang

- o   Jay Rozensweig
- o   Arianna Huffington
- o   Molly DeWolf
- o   Debra Messing
- o   Busy Phillips
- o   Carrie Byalik
- o   Andrew Lear and Natasha Boulouki
- o   Ashley Hoff
- o   Susanna Schrobensdorff
- o   Gillian Hormel
- o   Maria Shriver
- o   Kelly Clarkson
- o   Michele Smith (aka A Girl Has No President)
- o   Mandana Dayani
- Apostoli, Julia, Riko, Bobby, Katy, Ya-Ya, you are forever in my heart and a piece of me

And last but not least, Helen. I think of you every single day, and you have accompanied me on this journey every step of the way. I always feel your presence and listen intently to your messages. I hear your voice in my head in the moments that I am doubting myself or too tired to continue — you cheer me on and tell me to "keep going." I want to make you proud and make sure that you have a hand in all that I do. I miss you so much, sister.

About the Author

Shelly Tygielski, founder of the Pandemic of Love movement, is a self-care activist, community organizer, and mindfulness teacher who spent over two decades in the corporate world in an award-winning career. She left that world behind in 2016 to follow her heart and align her work in the world with her core values. She has been designated as one of the "powerful women in the mindfulness movement." Shelly is the cofounder of Partners in Kind, a purpose-in-production fund that develops and invests in social impact in entertainment projects that seek to create change and shift culture. She is currently working on her doctorate at the Lilly Family School of Philanthropy at Indiana University and is focusing her research on the democratization of philanthropy in America, centering on mutual aid. Her work has been featured in over one hundred media outlets, including segments for CNN Heroes and *The Kelly Clarkson Show*, as well as in *Oprah Daily*, *Forbes*, and *The Washington Post*. For five years, prepandemic, she led a community of over fifteen thousand meditators in Broward County, Florida. She currently lives between Asheville, North Carolina, and North Lake Tahoe, California. She enjoys playing guitar, engaging in board sports, and drinking craft cocktails.

She happily shares her life with her husband, Jason, and her son, Liam.